How to Beat Sir Humphrey

How to Beat Sir Humphrey

ANTONY JAY

Illustrations by Shaun Williams

LONG BARN BOOKS

PUBLISHED BY
LONG BARN BOOKS

Ebrington, Gloucestershire GL55 6NW

First published in this form 1997
10 9 8 7 6 5 4 3 2 1

Set in 11.25/13.75pt Monotype Bembo
Printed and bound by Redwood Books, Trowbridge, Wiltshire

ISBN 0 952 8285 1 0

ACKNOWLEDGMENT

The first port of call for anyone whose territory is threatened by bureaucratic or commercial developers is The National Sensitive Sites Alliance (see address index at the back of the book for details). It is run by Ian Martin, and his help in the preparation of this book has been invaluable.

CONTENTS

PREFACE

We all have to deal with bureaucrats and bureaucracies and it is a real pain. We are passed from ministry to town hall, from region to region, from department to department; our letters are not answered, our phone calls are not returned, our files go missing; the computer is down, the person we were dealing with is off sick, on leave or simply 'not at her desk' whenever we ring; our application arrived too late, the information is not available, we filled in the form incorrectly and we must re-apply after the start of the next financial year.

It seams like an unwinnable battle. **It is nothing of the kind**. Bureaucrats are immensely vulnerable in all sorts of ways and to pierce their armour all you need is some insight into their mental processes and a working knowledge of the tactics and techniques that will give you the best chance of victory. That is what this book sets out to provide.

It is not actually all that difficult. There are general principles (e.g. attack decisions, not people and always give officials an honourable way out) and there are rules for your guidance in specific skills such as telephone conversations (e.g. always get the name of the person you are talking to) writing letters (e.g. always write to the top person and address them by name), attending meetings, taking minutes, issuing press releases, holding press conferences, organising petitions, and the more specialist activities such as raising funds, reading between the lines of official documents and conducting public demonstrations.

In the following pages all these situations are examined and simple rules are given. The structure of the book follows the course of a typical major public protest, and I hope it will give a lot of practical help to all the people in communities whose lives are blighted by the threatened assault of planners and developers. Of course most of us, mercifully, are fighting less dramatic and less public battles. Nevertheless the course of a major protest brings in, at one point or another, all the principles and rules and techniques referred to above as well as giving the book a narrative progression; so I hope that whatever all your particular bureaucratic hassles and tussles may be you will find help in dealing with large organisations and gain insight into how bureaucrats fight their battles – and realise how you can take them on and beat them.

Eternal Vigilance

The crazy thing about protesting is that the time when you are most likely to succeed is the time when you are least likely to act. It is at the very beginning of the project that you have the best chance.

Put yourself in the enemy's mind for a moment. For our purposes let us make him one of the most formidable of enemies: Sir Humphrey himself – a government department – or a nationalised industry, or a local authority. This is not to say that private developers and commercial undertakings cannot be dangerous aggressors too: they have more money and better high-level contacts than you have, and full-time staff to work on the project. But they are not the final judges, and (at least in theory) you are both equal before the planning officers, the tribunals and the law courts. But when the enemy is the referee as well, when a government official will be adjudicating between you and an arm of government, or indeed when it has given initial planning consent to a private developer, then you have to fight ten times as hard for the same chance of success.

The very first stage is the broad intention: someone needs a motorway, an industrial estate, a gasholder, a pylon route, a refuse tip, a sewage farm, a superstore. There is very little you can do at this point. But once this decision has been taken, it has to be turned into a project, which means that one or more officials have to fix on a physical location. It is now that considerations come in.

Some of them are obvious: cost, access, convenience, efficiency and so on, and they will narrow the area of choice for the point of territorial aggression. But after them come the imponderables, like amenity value and community disruption, and now the slightly less honourable considerations appear. In particular, what will cause the officials least trouble? Does place A mean lengthy and complicated geological surveys? Does place B mean endless, boring discussions with the Ministry of Defence about releasing an artillery range? Is place C dangerously close to the Lord Lieutenant's pheasant shoot? Does place D mean drawing up a completely new set of plans and estimates, instead of digging the old ones out of the file? **What is wrong with place E – surely that's the answer?**

What is wrong with place E is that you live there, all unaware of the project and of the considerations revolving in official minds. If only you could find out now, you could try and indicate what was wrong with place E: namely, that it would cause a violent public outcry and a long-drawn-out, bitter battle against a well-organized, determined and vicious group of citizens. At this stage, when all the ideas are fluid and several alternatives are being mulled over, that new consideration might rule out place E without anything more being heard about it. But how can you find out that anything is being planned at all?

The short answer is that you can't. But if you keep your eyes and ears open you may get the occasional clue. Friends and neighbours working on the council, in estate agents' offices or for solicitors may sniff something in the wind. Rumours may start to circulate – don't discount the wild tales you hear in the local hairdresser's or newsagent's. Strangers may arrive in cars during working hours and stroll around looking. Most significant and urgent of all, young men with

theodolites, surveying poles and clip-boards may start to case the area.

None of these indicators can be ignored. **Do not wait until something firm is announced**: **firmness is the danger**. You must act urgently, and by telephone. Letters are useless at this stage – it is the menace, the tone of voice you are after. Some unscrupulous protesters use the standard journalistic technique of inventing an appalling story to get an informative denial ('No, it's utter nonsense – no one has ever even mentioned an urban motorway – the road-widening scheme is all that has ever been mooted.') Others exploit the poor communication and bad confidence between central and local government when inventing sources of information. ('I don't care what the ministry told you – the planning committee isn't even going to put it on the agenda until October.') It is even reported that people have succeeded in disguising their voices and pretended to be from the local authority when they phone the ministry.

('We keep being pestered by this boring little man who says you're going to build an open prison in his garden –

could you let us know what actually is being discussed?')
And of course you can play on the vanity of officials. ('Perhaps I could speak to someone senior enough to give me the information?')

All this may sound devious and tedious. So it is. But it is worth it if it enables you to whip up local frenzy before anything is finally decided, and nip the plans in the bud. But assuming you fail (and it is regrettably rare for plans to be forestalled in this way), then your enemy has appeared and you must organize your resistance: that is what this book is about.

PART ONE

The Initial Organization

I. Understand the Nature of the Plan

The enemy at this stage is not the council, the ministry, the officials or anyone else. **The enemy is the plan itself. When the plan is published, you will not regard it as a document at all, but as an act of naked, iron-fisted territorial aggression.** 'They' are going to run a six-lane dual carriageway past your bedroom window, build an electricity generating station on the village green, remove the shopping centre and replace it in four years' time with its soul removed, knock down your children's school, fell twenty great oak trees and replace them with fuchsias, and evict you while they think of what to do next. As you stand on the doormat and open the cheap manila envelope or see the

front page of the local paper, the words are blurred by the trembling of your hand and the drawings obscured by a red mist of anger. A cool appraisal of the merits of the plan is out of the question. All the same, a cool appraisal is essential; so wait till your heart stops thumping and your breathing returns to normal, and then sit down and study it carefully.

You will get nowhere unless you look at the plan from the standpoint of Sir Humphrey and his colleagues, the men who drew it up. They have been at it for months. It has generated several major internal rows. There have been long-negotiated compromises with other departments. The chap who started it all off was promoted halfway through and moved to Edinburgh. The first draft was produced in a tremendous rush because the Minister/Permanent Secretary/Chairman of the Planning Committee didn't give the go-ahead till three months after the deadline date, and some of the flaws didn't show up until it was too late to do anything. The policy decision it stems from was taken six years ago, and they're now talking about rethinking the whole policy on a more comprehensive basis, so if it does not go through quickly it may never make it. It has meant a great deal of work and unpleasantness and getting home late for supper, and the thought of going back to square one gives them all nightmares.

And yet, for all that, Sir Humphrey is proud of it: proud at least of having turned out such a plausible and workmanlike job in the face of all the difficulties. Of course it has flaws, but they are well disguised. Of course it will be attacked, but all plans are attacked. And on the whole, he has come to believe that as a practical project in an imperfect world it is probably the best one around. **To you it appears the product of an exhaustive and comprehensive survey from which unarguable facts lead by irresistible logic to inevitable conclusions**. **That is how it is**

meant to appear. **It is**, **however**, **exactly the reverse**. It started as a quick decision by a busy man several years ago. There was no time for more than a brief review of possibilities before that decision was taken. All work thereafter has been directed at making that early decision stand up. All the statistical analysis, the surveys, the expenditure forecasting, the projected growth of demand – these did not lead up to the choice at all: they were initiated and selected in order to bolster it up afterwards. They are rationalizations masquerading as reasons.

If you doubt this, reflect on London's third airport. The famous 1970 Roskill Commission took three million words of evidence from 160 people and organizations, it occupied the minds of nine eminent and impartial citizens for more than two and a half years, it produced a report backed up by nine volumes of research and testimony, and at the end of all that it was still possible for opponents to criticize its facts as inadequate and for the government to reject its conclusions as unacceptable. Can you believe that your plan has received one hundredth of the time, care and skill that went into Roskill? If you can, reflect on a further fact: the Roskill Commission grew from another government plan, Stansted. All the arguments and statistics, we were told, pointed inevitably to Stansted as the only conceivable choice. Minister after minister dutifully mouthed the words of his officials to explain why no other site was possible. But one of the first glaringly obvious conclusions reached by Roskill was that Stansted was such a bad choice as not to be worth even short-listing.

2. Understand the Nature of the Planners

The plan, therefore, is by no means the crushing and unanswerable fait accompli that it appears to you under the stress of that first emotional surge in your breast. And it is vulnerable in another way too: perhaps, for your purposes, an even more important way.

Just as the plan is meant to look unanswerable, so the authority behind it is meant to look indivisible. **You are meant to assume that all arms of government – national and local**, **public bodies and nationalized industries – together with all representatives of the people – ministers**, **MPs**, **chairmen of committees**, **county**, **borough and town councillors – are united in their resolve to implement the plan without modification and without delay**.

Nothing could be further from the truth. The plan is a patchwork of compromises; not just between political representatives anxious to avoid a fuss and officials anxious to avoid tiresome extra work, but between different departments of the council, different ministries, between town hall and Whitehall, and between various groups within those larger institutions. A few have already circulated their reservations about it: many more are keeping theirs to themselves for the time being.

It follows that the worst thing you can possibly do at this stage is to force them to declare a public alliance behind the plan. This is where far too many protesters lose the war before the first battle: to lump all these mutually suspicious rival interests together as 'pompous councillors and arrogant bureaucrats' ranks, for political wisdom, with Hitler's invasion of Russia or Japan's attack on Pearl Harbour. In their internal dissensions lie some of your best hopes; **you must do nothing that will make them close ranks**.

The first rule of protest, therefore, is to refrain from attacking any individual or group or official or department until you know precisely who your true enemies are. Your only implacable enmity at the moment is directed towards the plan itself: you should make it absolutely clear that it cannot, must not and will not happen. But even the councillor or official immediately responsible should not be singled out: you may yet persuade him to change his mind in the light of new evidence. Luther once appealed from 'the Pope badly advised' to 'the Pope well advised' and you may yet do the same with Councillor Higginson and his Chief Planning Officer.

3. The First Response

The first response to the plan is all-important. It has to be a public meeting, and it absolutely must be well attended. If only a handful of people turn up you may never recover from it; if you get a packed hall you have the beginnings of a great campaign. To maximize attendance:

• Book the hall and announce the date as quickly as possible. Your aim is to get the details of the meeting

announced in the two- or three-day burst of publicity that follows the publication of the plan.

- The date must be far enough ahead to give you the best chance of maximum attendance, but not so far that the first flush of anger will have been dissipated by the time it arrives: say about a week.

- Get as many people as you can to impress the urgency of a high attendance on their friends, but in particular work through existing organizations. Residents Associations, the Rotary Club, the Chamber of Trade, the WI, and the Townswomen's Guild, the Allotments Association, the area Neighbourhood Watch – any group that has a secretary and meets fairly regularly can save you precious hours of contact work.

- Have a placard-carrier outside the local supermarket at its busiest times, handing out leaflets summarizing the threat and giving the time and place of the meeting, and a parent distributing them among others waiting outside the gates of local schools at going-home time.

- Word-of-mouth publicity is probably even more effective than placards and leaflets. There are certain key locations that most people visit during a week – pubs, corner shops and local post offices, petrol stations – and a busy ally behind the counter to drum up attendance in each of them is worth a hundred letterbox leaflets.

- Pull out all the stops to get the most important and influential person you can to preside at the meeting: if he or she will address it as well, so much the better, but their name and presence are enough at this stage.

- Your local paper, radio and even television stations will probably get to hear of the meeting, but leave nothing to chance. Make sure they have plenty of notice and full details.

★

By far the most important function of this first meeting is to demonstrate the size and strength of the opposition to the plan. The size has already been discussed: the strength will emerge at the meeting, and you must make sure it has the opportunity.

- This particular meeting is an emotional one, and you cannot make it into anything else. Nor do you want to. It is about how people feel.
- You must, nevertheless, use accurate facts. The value of popular feeling can be undermined later if it transpires that the meeting was misled. So when you outline what the plan will mean to the neighbourhood, do not misrepresent it.
- Popular support is your only real weapon, so make sure as many different people as possible have their say, even if only to ask questions.
- Visible unanimity is important, audible unanimity even more so. Better to shout out, 'Do we accept the plan?' and get a roar of, 'No!' than ask for a show of hands: that can come later. If you reach the pitch where the whole audience sings 'We shall not be moved' (or 'Jerusalem' – or 'Three Blind Mice' for that matter) you are well and truly on your way.
- Prepare everyone for the idea that they may be called on for their help – not just knocking at doors and addressing envelopes, but advice or skilled work as well. Then take everyone's names and addresses and telephone numbers as they leave – (twenty sixth-formers at the exits with pencil and paper) – and also their profession, trade, special skill or hobby.
- The only practical result required from the meeting is that it should authorize the organizers of the meeting to form

an Action Committee to speak on their behalf, and to report back at the next meeting.

• As people leave, ask them to make a first financial contribution to the fighting fund.

4. Building a Command Structure

Who should serve on the Action Committee? This is an extremely delicate and sensitive decision, and one which can be embarrassing or even impossible to recover from if you get it wrong. It is appallingly unfair that you should have to take it so early. There is, however, a clear principle and there are also various useful dodges.

The principle is that the Action Committee should comprise only the best people for the job. We will discuss what this means in a moment: for the time being it is enough to say that, as the name implies, they must all be active and committed. The delicacy of the decision springs from the number of people who do not qualify, and yet are valuable allies and will be offended, perhaps mortally, if they are not invited to join.

This is where the dodges come in. There must be no compromises over the Action Committee, but you can invent all sorts of other imposing institutions for the honour and glory of those you exclude. You can have a community council to whom you formally report once a quarter. You can have an advisory council and a number of consultative committees. When the community council grows too large to be an honour, you can restore the dignity of the more senior by making them vice-presidents. That still leaves you the valuable title of 'Patron' in reserve for the local bigwigs. It may seem petty and unworthy, but the power of these names and symbols is not to be despised: a

good worker who is flagging can take on a new lease of life when invited to join an honorific body.

5. Choosing the Action Committee

From now on the success of your protest depends on the Action Committee. What does it have to do?

First of all, it has to choose a leader, someone deeply committed to the cause, dynamic and clear-headed. They will have to be good at dealing with the media and happy to delegate, able to think strategically, not afraid of confrontation but not confrontation-seekers either. The owner of a local small business has often turned out to be a good choice. They will be the face of the action group as seen by the outside world.

But you also need a deputy leader, or even a joint leader. They are the face of the action group as seen by those who are part of it. As the leader looks outwards to the world, so the deputy or joint leader looks inwards to the group. They are persuasive, diplomatic and charming, but with a steel centre. They keep up the enthusiasm, strengthen the flagging, praise the deserving and resolve internal tension and conflict. Experience, which is immune to charges of sexism, suggests that men are more often found as the outward-lookers and women as the inward-lookers, but there is no 100 per cent rule.

Next, you have to face the fact that there is too much work for a single committee to undertake on its own. In fact your campaign, as we shall see, has to proceed simultaneously on seven fronts, and each needs a specialized small team, or cell, to carry out the work. You must choose as your Action Committee the seven specialists who will form and lead these teams. In fact you will probably have two or three already: the group which called the meeting is likely to contain the nucleus. They will probably know one or two other possibles, and the remainder will require several exploratory discussions. For all the urgency of getting things going, it is better to wait than to make in haste what you sense instinctively may be an unfortunate decision. If you do pick wrongly, you absolutely must put the mistake right the moment you admit it to yourselves. If you wait, it gets harder and more awkward every day. You will end up severing with friction and un-pleasantness a relationship which could have ended grace-fully a fortnight earlier by a promotion to the community council: '. . . as an undercover agent for the Action Committee, to keep them sweet and stop them meddling.'

The first meeting of the Action Committee has to make some basic decisions about strategy: do we want utter rejection of the plan, or will we accept modifications? If we will accept modifications, should we say so now or keep it back until later? It must also be made clear that the target is victory, not martyrdom. Better to stop the plan undramatically and quietly than goad authority into forcing it through in a blaze of national publicity. Twyford Down and the Newbury by-pass did nobody any good.

To keep up the impetus, no meeting should ever be adjourned without fixing a date for the next one and making sure everyone has a project, however simple and brief, to complete and report on. **The project at the first meeting is for every member to form his cell and bring their names to the next meeting**, **especially the name of his deputy**.

6. The Creation of the Cells

You are fighting an enemy with massive resources and vast statutory powers, **and you have little enough of either**. **You are in the position of a guerrilla force**, **and you must use guerrilla tactics**: small groups, carefully worked out targets, concealment, surprise, dedication, strong local support, skill, ingenuity, cunning and a flexible, informal organisation. The guerrilla bands, the cells, need all these, and their success depends on a full utilization of the best skills of the community. Few communities are aware of the wealth of these human resources until they come under pressure, but they must all be mobilized quickly: lawyers, accountants, advertising men, journalists, architects, surveyors, university lecturers – they can transform a local protest from an emotional spasm into a formidable counter-attack. The cells can almost operate independently, but in fact their strength is much increased if their work is properly coordinated when the leaders meet on the Action Committee to plan a concerted movement.

7. The First Cell: Grass Roots

It must never be forgotten that this is the whole neighbourhood's united opposition, **not just the protest of a few NIMBY busybodies**. You therefore have to keep in touch with everyone, and make sure they feel they are part of the protest. You can only do this by a network of street and area representatives. It is very possible that there is an existing organization you can work through – a Residents', Tenants' or Ratepayers' Association, or a Neighbourhood Watch. If not, you must build it. Two hundred houses is about the maximum any representative can look after, and then only if they have a great deal of energy, devotion and spare time. Fifty is more likely, and twenty or thirty is acceptable with someone who wants to help but would be daunted by too demanding an assignment. This is where the telephone numbers come in: a 'chain' telephone network can spread information rapidly, with no one having to make more than half a dozen calls.

Never have more than ten street representatives to an area committee. If your numbers expand, you can multiply the levels – district committees, regional committees, etc. – but you must never break the rule of ten. And of course it applies all the way up – no more than ten area representatives to a district committee, no more than ten district representatives to a regional committee. You can of course appoint area, district and regional councils to give you another clutch of dignified sinecures to dispose of at a slightly lower level, but like the campaign council they are honorary and advisory. Don't let them clutter up the business meetings.

The first place to look for your potential representatives is the list of names and addresses you took at the first meeting. Obviously you want to cover the widest possible area. **There are stories that some protest groups have boosted**

recruiting in communities who thought the plan did not affect them by sending a couple of lads with a theodolite and surveying pole to spend the morning taking bearings and replying, 'I'm sorry, I can't tell you,' to all inquiries about who they were and what they were doing: I cannot vouch for this, however.

8. The Second Cell: Funds

It is a poignant irony that the massive resources of central and local government come from your taxes and your rates, just as their authority comes from your votes. Nevertheless, a first-class protest can fail for lack of a few hundred pounds, and so you have to raise more money to fight the money you have already handed over to the enemy.

You will obviously collect all you can from the grass roots, but you will be lucky if this does more than cover your running costs and expenses. If counsel has to be briefed for an inquiry, or if civil action has to be taken in the courts, you are in the fund-raising business, which is quite different. Fund-raising at this level is not about collecting small sums from large numbers: it is after large sums from small numbers.

The detailed techniques will be discussed later, **but there is one fund-raising device you can employ straight away which may raise a surprisingly large sum very quickly**: **an auction**. You will be astonished at the volume and variety of saleable goods that your supporters can bring forward once they have the light of battle in their eye and the scent of victory in their nostrils. Urge them to ransack wardrobes and lumber rooms, lofts and cellars, garages and cupboards under the stairs, and bring along all the pictures and ornaments they never look at, the glass and china they never use, the impossible wedding presents and unbearable Christmas presents, and heap them all up in one great act of sacrifice to the cause. A local estate agent/auctioneer will advise you, and probably conduct the auction for nothing. You will almost certainly get a good attendance, even if only from curiosity about what the neighbours have been hoarding all these years, and it is by no means impossible to raise a five-figure sum, and get the fighting fund off to a flying start.

Two useful ways of raising funds allied to this are worth outlining. (Of course, your Fund-Raising cell will come up with dozens of other ideas when they get their heads together.)

If you have to begin in the depths of winter, people may want to help and like the idea of an auction, but may not be so keen on leaving their warm firesides then, for an evening's bidding in a draughty hall. There will also be those who simply do not have anything much to donate – perhaps they have recently moved house, and so already had their grand clearout, perhaps they have simply never been hoarders, but they may well be just as keen to help in any way they can. Do not spurn them. You need all the enthusiasm and energy you can tap into. Not everyone will have things to offer, but what about services? A morning's ironing, an evening's babysitting, a batch of home-baked pies and cakes or even an entire dinner for the freezer: a chauffeured car trip to a shopping centre, and a couple of stalwarts to carry the resultant bags and parcels – this is an offer likely to prove most attractive to the elderly, the car-less or the disabled, who would like to go further afield, with help, perhaps in the weeks before Christmas. A few dozen lots of this kind listed together is called an Auction of Promises, and of course you can hold it in the same way as you hold your auction of objects. **But if it is indeed the depths of a bad winter, and yet mat-**

ters are urgent, you can't risk leaving your fund-raising until the warmer, lighter nights: so hold an Armchair Auction. It works very simply and straightfor-wardly, with one person working as co-ordinator. You invite offers of promises – this is probably the hardest part, but you will find that once the idea gets around, many people will be generous with their suggestions and their time, and also lead you to other potential donors. It is essential to have one or two really valuable promises – perhaps a day's clay-pigeon shooting, or a hot-air balloon flight. Be bold – contact local businesses and ask what they might offer, and always speak to the Managing Director, or as near as you can get to them. If necessary, make an appointment to call back when they will be available. The girl on the switchboard may be charming and as helpful as she knows how, but she has no power or authority to promise a free trip in the Chairman's helicopter.

When you have all your offers, list them, starting with the most valuable or even bizarre, to grab attention but then mixing them carefully, so that Mr Smith is not hurt when his offer to re-pot houseplants – likely to raise no more than a fiver – is relegated to the bottom, below even the Playgroup's offer of mustard-and-cress grown to order (bidder to supply the flannel.)

Someone with access to a computer can print off a large number of the lists and they are distributed house-to-house, inserted as a flyer in the local community paper, handed out after club and society meetings, church services, left on shop counters and in the pub and so on. In your brief introduction above the list, you invite bids and ask for the forms to be returned with the bids clearly marked beside the lots and names, with addresses and telephone numbers added, by a given date. The lists could be delivered, posted or faxed to you, and you could also put special posting-boxes in local shops, the pub, the club, the church, and so on. People greatly enjoy browsing through such a selection of offers without the trouble of leaving hearth and home to bid for what they want – they do it from their armchair and they do not need to view the promise of a morning's ironing as they would naturally wish to inspect the iron and ironing board that might be on offer in a normal auction. The co-ordinator's job is on the whole a straightforward one. A few lots will have attracted no bids at all – perhaps a tour of the local beauty spots on the back of a young enthusiast's motorbike might not have been fiercely competed for even in summer weather and possibly Mrs Murgatroyd's offer of A Musical Entertainment for your Party or Family Gathering has been given a wide berth by all who may have heard her sing and play at the annual Parish Concert. But the offers of a morning's housework or an afternoon's gardening have proved very popular, and everyone wants two dozen of Mrs Baker's mince-pies and sausage rolls, delivered warm to the house. The co-ordinator treats these in exactly the same way as the auctioneer treats the most desirable items on his table in the hall: they go to the highest bidder. What if there are four identical bids? This is where the co-ordinator's silver tongue and skills of persuasion come in. The four bidders are telephoned in turn and the 'auctioneer' starts wheedling a higher bid out of them. Naturally, there is a good deal of 'Now, I'm sorry I can't tempt you just a little higher than that, Mrs Jones. I can't? Sure? Yet a mere fifty pence more would secure it for you over Mrs Robinson . . .' Of course, Mrs Jones goes the extra fifty pence. The co-ordinator should not be tempted to lie, or even embroider the truth at this stage even with the best intentions. If Mrs Jones discovers, on lingering behind to chat at the school gate after dropping off little Johnny the next day, that Mrs Robinson certainly did not bid anywhere near that amount for the Two Afternoons of Dog Walking, feelings will run very high indeed and the probity of the auctioneer and the handling of the entire auction may be called into question. Nevertheless, when properly conducted, this is an efficient and very enjoyable method of fund-raising, particularly in a local community with well-defined boundaries – a large village, say, or a small estate.

If a rough field, or school playground or parish hall car-park can be borrowed for a Saturday afternoon or Sunday morning, hold a car-boot sale. The police will have to be notified, and traffic management carefully planned in advance and well-directed on the day – your retired military men come into their own here; widely publicized car boot sales can attract a very great many cars indeed and the last thing you can afford is to come into conflict with the law. Any goods that have failed to attract bids at the auction can be offered for sale by a volunteer willing to stand outside in the cold, and very probably wet, for a few hours. But the real money raised by a car boot sale comes from renting out the pitches to visiting car-booters, many of whom are regulars, or even semi-professionals, who go round from site to site every weekend, and who make very good second-incomes from trading. They expect to pay the going rate for a pitch and count it as part of their normal expenses. Charge a few pounds more for cars turning up on the day than for those which have been booked in beforehand. Given good advance advertising, a large, easy-to-find site and a fine day, you can certainly expect to make several hundred pounds. If a few of your volunteers are willing to run a refreshment stall, with hot and soft drinks, good home-made filled rolls and cakes, your takings will be even higher.

Other useful fund-raising devices include holding barbecues, dances and discos and country-and-western evenings, and selling T-shirts, sweatshirts, coffee mugs and baseball caps with the action group's name on. If you can call on the services of a graphic artist, or art teacher with the same kind of flair, you might consider having a logo and slogan for the campaign – something simple and striking – and print those on the merchandise you're selling too.

But if you are thinking of making a street (shaking tins) or house-to-house collection, **a word of warning**. **The bye-laws governing these are extremely strict – and strictly enforced**. Always contact the police and your local council for advice before taking any decisions, and remember, too, that even if you are granted a licence for, say, a street collection, there are a limited number of Saturdays on which you would find it at all profitable to hold them (generally between late April and October but excluding August), and these are usually booked up well ahead by the large national Charities. The rules governing house-to-house collections are even more stringent. But you may find it worthwhile to get permission from local private shops to put your 'official' collecting tins on their counters. You should not expect to raise large sums this way though, and must give meticulously accurate, individual receipts to be displayed in each store after the boxes have been emptied.

9. The Third Cell: Law

The Action Committee badly needs at least one qualified lawyer. You are playing a game with complicated rules, and the rules are tucked away in any number of judgments and statute books. It is not enough to have good legal advice when you can afford it: **you need a cell**, **headed by a lawyer**, **thinking hard all the time about the legal side of the campaign**. If you have no lawyer available, try and find a fairly senior solicitor's clerk or an ex-adjutant. Failing that, you may find you have a natural amateur lawyer in the community. Colin Seymour of Flamborough in Yorkshire has no legal training but in 1997 he won his 81st successive case against the authorities using a 1765 enclosure law to stop the council uprooting a hedge.

10. The Fourth Cell: Influential Allies

This must be headed by your chairman – not to be confused with the leader of the Action Committee. **The chairman should be the most respected and influential person who is committed to your cause**. It is the Chairman's job to use the old-boy net to land the biggest fish in the district. In rural areas these are likely to be Lord Lieutenants, peers, knights, dames, elder statesmen, retired judges, generals, permanent secretaries and captains of industry – all the names worth dropping. In city areas there may be fewer of those ready to join in, but more school governors, health authority members, industrialists, magistrates, small business proprietors and senior members of voluntary organisations.

The rest of the cell are responsible for finding out and contacting all the people and organizations, local and national, which might be on your side.

11. The Fifth Cell: The Experts

This cell contains the storm troops of your attack on the plan. You need professional people: architects, surveyors, accountants, high-level civil servants, planners and top managers from large corporations, university lecturers, consultants, scientists. All of them should have personal secretaries, or access to secretarial facilities. Their task is to attack the plan on its own terms. Since it has been produced by professionally qualified people with trained minds, you need the same skills. Quite probably you have better ones than they have in some areas, though you are unlikely to have the whole dream team listed above. Even so, you have one important advantage – the dedicated passion of citizens protecting their homeland from the invader.

The Experts' Cell will not be short of work. In practice, you will probably not be able to command sufficient experts to explore every possible opening. Nevertheless you may well have sufficient to shoot gaping holes in the plan, and once people realize the tasks to be done you may be surprised at the quality of support you can call on. **All sorts of people who cannot raise much enthusiasm for addressing envelopes and collecting signatures may be stimulated by the prospect of proving themselves in expert technical combat with the ministry or the town hall**.

Remember that people respond better to the idea of a defined project than general service to a cause. If you can start the cell off with just three or four people, their first investigations can be designed to make preliminary surveys of promising lines of attack. Once you have a precise brief, you can call on the neighbouring surveyor or accountant or geography professor much more easily, and with the much more powerful argument that it absolutely has to be them and no one else.

12. The Sixth Cell: Publicity

For publicity read politics. Hardly any protests directly involve enough voters to disturb the electoral security of a single borough councillor, let alone an MP; but once the affair gets into the press and radio and television, a much wider spread of voters will be influenced by the actions and words of the council or the government. **Your object is to start MPs and councillors wondering whether the railroading of this plan is worth the possible cost of their seats**: the risk may be slight, but their affection for the plan may also be slight. If you can only break into the media you can open up a whole new battlefield, and one on which you do not fight at a disadvantage.

13. The Seventh Cell: Campaign Headquarters

'Headquarters' is perhaps too grand a name for what will probably be the front room of a private house. Nevertheless you cannot run the campaign without a fixed base. You need a telephone that is manned all day, and with an efficient answerphone back-up; you need a fax machine, you need an address for delivery of leaflets from the printers or computer-owning members; you need a bulletin board to display dates and announcements and press cuttings, and you need a place where you can count on an easy chair and a cup of tea.

The campaign director, who is Chairman of the Action Committee, will use it as a base, but as an admiral using it as the flagship, not the captain of the ship. Ideally, the headquarters will be run by a husband-and-wife team, or other domestic partnership. One of them must be a fixer. This is a quite distinct and recognizable skill. I am not sure where you go to find it, though it is common among, for example, television floor managers and army quartermasters; its exponents have a marvellous gift for improvising, for persuading people, for getting unlikely permissions and extracting free facilities, and they are at their best when disaster strikes at the eleventh hour. They will borrow for you a string of polo ponies, have the police divert traffic for you, get permission to use St. James's Park for your parade, or St. Paul's Cathedral for your thanksgiving service after the public inquiry. With a good fixer, tea and coffee and drinks always appear when they are wanted, locked doors open, transport appears on demand, and the only price you have to pay is small cash sums at irregular intervals, without asking questions. The other skill is indefatigability; the willingness to try the engaged number for the seventh time, to keep at Mr Jones for the minutes and Mr Smith for the copies of his letters and Ms Brown for the results of the door-to-door survey, to work steadily down a long list of tasks, chasing other people's progress with charm, cheerfulness and relentless determination. Of course, it does not have to be a couple, but a constant awareness of what the other is up to does enormously strengthen the cell: indeed, if a skilled fixer teams up with an indefatigable chaser there is almost nothing the partnership cannot achieve.

The Headquarters Cell does, however, have a special responsibility beyond making sure that all the other cells perform the tasks set by the Action Committee: it is the cell that conducts all preliminary and exploratory negotiation with officials, councillors, MPs and other influential people and groups. For this you will need at least one first-class salesman – more than one if possible – with that special salesman's gift of sensing people's attitudes, their vanities and weaknesses and strong points of resolution, and the marvellous capacity for turning himself into just the sort of person the other person most likes, however conflicting the tastes of the others he has to deal with. And since the cell is the focus of all information, the local gossip and nosy parker will also be valuable.

PART TWO

Campaign Tactics

The Action Committee has been constituted. and its members have picked the teams that will form the nucleus of their cells. Each cell must clearly understand its task and know how to set about it. Work must begin straight away, before the initial impetus is lost.

I. Mobilizing the Grass Roots

The primary purpose of the grass-roots organization is to ensure maximum turn-out whenever you want to stage a public meeting or event, or stimulate any other mass activity, like writing to the MP or collecting signatures. But a lively organization can do much more. It can underpin the work of three other cells: Headquarters, Publicity and Funds. It is a sensitive information network, by which every little fact or rumour about the enemy's actions comes straight to headquarters. It is a source of good tactical ideas for protest marches and demonstrations. It can mobilize an impressive fleet of transport at short notice. It will turn up all sorts of hidden talents – the poster artist, the cartoonist to liven up the circulars, the inspired improvising carpenter for the floats. Sometimes it can unearth an invaluable resource – a photocopier, computers, a loud-hailer, lengths of chain for 'the march of the slaves' past the town hall. And of course the monthly 50p or one pound subscription keeps the fighting fund topped up.

But none of this will appear unless it is sought. So there must be regular meetings of representatives in which they are kept fully informed of latest moves and developments and plans, and asked for specific ideas and help, and told of the chief problems and shortages. The more they suggest and propose themselves, and the more it is their ideas which are being implemented by the Action Committee rather than vice versa, the stronger the roots of the protest. **Remember that protest is not a steady activity**: **it has crests and troughs**. **The first crest is at the time of the very first meeting**, **and you have to catch it quickly to get the organization set up**, **and have early meetings for all the representatives**. They should be sent away with a task – the best one is to introduce themselves to the households they represent, and make a sort of inventory of skills, resources and general willingness to turn out for meetings.

It should be made clear to all of them that steady hard work is not required. Their purpose is to be available when

projects demand it. They must not find it tedious; they need the stimulus of a target date – the big meeting, the march, the public inquiry, the bring-and-buy, the protest exhibition – to work for, so that they can make an effort and then relax until next time. Part of the Action Committee's job is to make sure that these crests occur frequently enough – every three months or so in a long campaign – to keep the organization muscular and flexible.

In the troughs, all that is needed is regular distribution of information, the duplicated news-sheet that gives the state of battle, news of any support from outside sources, and brief accounts of what the different groups and areas are working at. If distribution is a problem, local newsagents might agree to help by giving one out with each morning paper, either over the counter or in the delivery.

2. Raising the Wind

Fund-raising has become a thriving business in recent years, with any number of techniques to support it. All of it, however, is based on a few simple principles, and once your Fund-Raising Cell has got hold of them they should have little difficulty in applying them to individual cases.

- The fund needs a precise objective. 'The Fighting Fund' is all very well for the first wave of fear and resentment, but it is a collection box idea, not a fund-raising idea. A precise objective is something like briefing counsel, or printing an illustrated booklet to circulate to MPs, or commissioning a survey of an alternative route or site.
- The objective must seem worth the money to the people you approach. Everyone in the cell must therefore be convinced of its importance themselves before they call on

anyone, and if they are questioned they must be able to explain why it is essential.

- The precise total sum required must be stated, and it must be the maximum you think you can get. Too large, and you lose credibility at the start and depress morale as the appeal goes on. Too small, and you have missed a golden opportunity. An expert friend of mine was horrified when, at a public dinner to launch a national campaign, the organizer asked for \$12,000. He was horrified because there was at least a quarter of a million pounds sitting round the table, and he could almost hear the minds clicking as the guests scaled down the cheques they had come prepared to write.

- Because the precise target figure is so important, take some soundings first. Ask some of the keenest supporters among the people you will be approaching for their advice on what seems a worthy cause to go fund-raising for, and tell them the sort of costs you look like having to meet. Show them your provisional appeal-figure with a breakdown of how you hope to achieve it – (one gift of £5,000, two of £2,500, four of £1,000, five hundred of £10) and ask them where they might come in that list. For details of the approach technique, see (vi) and (vii) below.

  Divide the list into two with a space line as shown in the table, and put the space line below the minimum figure you expect your survey group to subscribe: many who were thinking of fifty pounds will suddenly decide to make it one hundred in order to get themselves above the great divide. On the basis of these soundings, review the target sum and see if it now looks too large – or too small.

- Start at the top. **Decide which individual (and which company and society too**, **if you are approaching groups) is going to make the largest single contribution**, **go to them before you approach anyone**

else and put your cards on the table. Explain that everyone else will scale down their contribution from the top and the more they cough up, the more everyone else will. A really large dollop from the top person reverberates throughout the whole subscription list and is worth ten times its face value. Show them your Donation Table, so that they are left in no doubt as to the sums you are talking about. Better still, show them two tables, one starting at £5,000, say, and the other at £10,000, so that they can see the total difference that is at stake.

			£		£
I	donation of		5,000	. . . .	5,000
4	"	"	2,500	. . . .	10,000
6	"	"	1,500	. . . .	9,000
12	"	"	1,000	. . . .	12,000
25	"	"	500	. . . .	12,500
50	"	"	250	. . . .	12,500
200	"	"	100	. . . .	20,000
500	"	"	50	. . . .	25,000
1,000	"	"	20	. . . .	20,000
2,400	"	"	10	. . . .	24,000

EXAMPLE OF DONATION TABLE

TOTAL 150,000

• Raise funds by having one member of the cell call on one potential contributor at a time, by previous arrangement. Postal appeals raise practically nothing, and group appeals are a complicated situation which requires experience. The strength of the one-to-one situation is that it creates a productive tension. The potential contributor, on the surface level of the interview, wants to help the cause but does not want to impoverish himself: this is the simple, surface tension. It is below the surface that the stronger tension operates; he is concerned for his status in the community as expressed by the amount of his contribution. This concern is the foundation of all successful fund-raising and the rest of the principles are built on it.

- The Fund-Raising Cell should comprise members who span the whole income range of the people they will call on, and members should only call on people who are more or less their financial equals. If there is a significant

difference, it makes it not only socially uncomfortable to talk about money, but inefficient too. With someone better off than you are, you hesitate to ask for a sum greater than you would contribute yourself: with someone less well off, a nice social discretion calls forth a similar reluctance to maximize. With an equal, there is the unspoken thought that if you can chip in that much, so can they. People who subscribe generously can later be recruited to call on others, as the appeal begins to spread its net wider.

- While you do not make the size of individual contributions available to the general public, you do not keep them a total secret internally, unless specifically asked to do so. You will find that many of those who ask for anonymity are happy to think that people in the community whose esteem they value are likely to know how much they put themselves down for. After all, virtue should not go unrecognized.

- Remember that the contributors that you call on may be wildly uncertain about how much you expect them to give. You have a duty to relieve them of anxiety. Judicious disclosures of sums guaranteed by others, or of the sum you have put up yourself, can help them there.
- Be prepared to name actual sums of money, and remember that the most common error is to make them too small. You must use tact, but firmness: 'Well, of course, any contribution is welcome and we are grateful for all we get. On the other hand it's no good pretending we've got much hope of reaching the target if people like us aren't prepared to go in for more than ten or twenty quid. It would be absolutely marvellous if we felt we could call on you for a hundred and fifty pounds – a hundred now and fifty later if we're in trouble. But' – if you pick up signs of anxiety – 'the basic one hundred pounds is what we need, or' – if the signs continue – 'fifty now and fifty standby, anyway'. If you're playing it by ear, you can come down more easily than you can go up, though going up can be achieved by experts. **Remember the optician's advice to his son**: **'Tell the customer, "That'll be fifty pounds" and pause for a fraction. If he doesn't flinch, say, "For the frames. The lenses are another fifty" and a tiny pause, then "Each."'**
- Every significant contributor must receive a letter of thanks, not from a committee but from the most respected figure in the campaign. Under pressure the letter itself can

be typed but it must be topped and tailed by the great man in his own hand. This is more than civilized courtesy: such a letter is always mentioned (incidentally, of course) in conversation, and hearing of it acts as a valuable stimulus to the waverers.

Fund-raising is about cash and should not be deflected. The only acceptable alternatives are the facilities and services you would have to spend cash on – printing work from a printer, a day's survey and report from a surveyor, six hours' of a typist's time plus free photocopying. But on the whole it is wise to keep off this area in the main fund-raising drive and wait until you actually need the service before you discuss alternatives to cash. You may even get it as an addition instead of an alternative.

3. The Law's Delay

You should not expect the Legal Cell to win the war. They might, and it will be wonderful if they do because a technical legal victory is the best kind of victory: it saves a great deal of time, trouble and acrimony. But their main value is more likely to be as a support arm than as a fighting arm – and it is support without which you cannot win.

- The Legal Cell must tell you how the game is played. Can you object? Can you force an inquiry? Is it possible to appeal? Who has to approve the plan? By what date? Does an elected body have to vote on it? Until you know the answers to all the questions like these you cannot really plan the rest of the campaign; equally, once you have the whole course of the proceedings mapped out, certain key points will stand out as occasions when specific action has to be taken, and the pattern of crests and troughs will begin to take shape. The government produces Planning Policy Guideline notes (PPGs) and local authorities have structure plans and it is on these that decisions on planning permission have to be based. They will obviously be the starting point for the Legal Cell, but they need to be checked regularly because nowadays they are being changed more and more frequently.

- They should watch like hawks for any legal mistakes by the enemy, for any failure to give proper notice, any demand or decision beyond their powers, any technical errors that may invalidate documents, any ambiguity or slovenliness in phrasing which may be valuable later.

- They must keep you aware of all your rights, and ensure you have access to all documents and plans to which you are entitled. They must alert you to all the situations in which you might have grounds for legal action or claims for compensation. In short, they must make sure you do not miss any opportunities because you are not sure of your legal position.

- The authorities are usually well aware of the basic laws relating to their plan, but they may be caught unawares on less familiar territory: local laws, footpaths, ancient lights, church land, restrictive covenants – the cell should explore all these.

- **Delaying tactics**. **These may prove to be the most valuable of all**. **Time is on your side**: as the months drag by, the enemy loses impetus. Some of them start to lose confidence and enthusiasm too. Officials who worked out the plans are moved to other jobs and other places. **Every week you delay is a week you gain. Some protesters even miss simple points like always objecting on the last possible day and not the first**, and so **they give the enemy weeks or months of the time**

they need for themselves. Lawyers have a sound understanding of the techniques of delay, and if the Legal Cell
applies itself creatively to the problem they should do you
proud.

4. The Big Guns

This is a job calling for experience, perseverance and tact:
probably the best people for it are those with past experience
as personal secretaries. Knowing how to write persuasive
letters to impersonal organizations is important too.

The 'Influential Allies' Cell must start immediately on
compiling the list of people and organizations who could be
called on to help; once the decisions have been made about
whom to approach, they have to decide when. At once?
When there is support from others? After some funds have
been raised? When there is a decent file of press cuttings? It
is usually better to start with the local organizations, the easier ones where personal approaches are possible, and with
the smaller national ones. Do not rush straight off to the
really influential heavyweights like the National Trust and
the Fine Art Commission: wait till you have substantial evidence from others that your case is worth supporting.

In principle, the Great Man should sign all these letters
himself, though most of them will be drafted for him by the
cell. They must find out something about the organization
first, so that the letter can be seen as more than a tired routine circular: 'Knowing of Lord Byway's interest in urban
problems . . .'; 'After your skilful and gallant defence of
Bedsyde Manor . . .'; '. . . feel we are the sort of people your
founder had in mind when he gave his famous inaugural lec-
ture in 1871 . . .'

You will know all the local bodies, the Rotary and the

Chamber of Commerce and the Women's Institute: after them come the Civic Trust, English Nature, The CPRE, Friends of the Earth, the Royal Institute of British Architects, the Victorian Society, the Georgian Society, the Historic Church Trust, the Society for the Preservation of Ancient Buildings, the Architectural Association, the Institute of Town Planning, the National Playing Fields Association, The Royal Society for the Protection of Birds, the Ramblers' Association, the Inland Waterways Association, the Consumers' Association, the Noise Abatement Society, the National Council for Civil Liberties – the list goes on and on, and the cell must approach every one that could possibly be of use. Many of them have journals, and a letter to the editor can make a good start.

Ideally they should ask for 100 per cent support and a contribution to the fighting fund, but if that is clearly not going to be forthcoming the request can be scaled down. Even if the organizations are too cagey to comment on your case, you may at least extract a general statement of principle which helps your case and swells your list of quotations. Better still, ask them to make their own inquiries on your behalf: **every letter that comes down to the enemy headquarters from a high level is a blow to your cause**.

It is of course extremely unwise to attract the support of one political party unless you can also involve the other. **Your grass-roots support is all-party**, **and if it gets about that the protest is in fact a one-party manoeuvre you will suffer irreparable damage**. The exception would be one of those rare issues like comprehensive schools, in which genuine party political conflict replaces the normal battle between the government and the people.

5. The Attack On the Concept

This is one of the three lines of attack to be taken by the Experts' Cell. It is the cell most likely to win the battle outright, and the plan is its battlefield. Indeed, if you can muster the strength, there is enough work to keep three Experts' Cells hard at it, one for each line of attack. This is an area in which The Internet can be very helpful. Most of the leading environmental organisations have Websites, and specific information and guidance can be sought by means of a newsgroup or bulletin board. But **be careful of canvassing support for campaign events on the net**; **it has sometimes proved to be a magnet for professional eco-warriors spoiling for a fight**.

The attack on the concept is a job for the best academic and theoretical thinkers you can find. They have to hack away at the intellectual foundations on which the plan is built. There are certain lines of inquiry which should prove fruitful.

- Is the plan necessary at all? Will it solve the problem it sets out to solve, or aggravate it, or create other, greater problems? This proved a valuable line of attack in the case of London's third airport – did London in fact need a third airport at all? A doubt cast at this level is a very grave doubt. Moreover, this is likely to be one of the weakest points in the enemy case – it is probably that sketchily verified hunch on which the whole plan was initiated.

- Has the plan taken into account all the most advanced thinking, the most recent experience, the latest technologies? Have the Japanese developed a new cheap way of burying electricity cables? Did the Rotterdam City Council solve the same traffic problem in a much better way last year? Has the Swedish architectural institution demonstrated the damage that this sort of plan can do to the community? The field of inquiry is broad and fertile, and examples from foreign countries have a special glamour as well as probably being unknown to the enemy, and hard for them to verify.

- Is the plan comprehensive enough? Has it considered the needs of the area as a whole? Has it taken into account future plans for schools, hospitals, shopping precincts? Almost certainly it has not: it is probably the product of rather narrow thinking by a single department. Everyone knows how the same piece of road can be dug up four times in four weeks by the gas people, the water people, the highways people and the electricity people, and exactly the same thing happens all the way up.

- Does the plan conflict with a broader regional plan? Can you argue that it should be delayed until the revised regional plan is published? This is technically known as 'prematurity' and has satisfactorily scuppered a lot of development proposals. Or is there an area of inconsistency or conflict between local government and national government which you can exploit – e.g. is the council planning a housing density or plot ratio which the ministry says is no longer acceptable for residential areas? Have new principles been formulated (e.g. about proximity of pedestrians to traffic) since the plan was drawn up, which make it invalid?

• Has there been proper consultation? Almost certainly there has not been proper advance consultation with the community affected, but the enemy will say that the councillors represent the community and it is the council's plan. But they may well have failed to consult (a) other bodies who are supposed to benefit, like shopkeepers, or (b) experts like consulting engineers, or (c) welfare and housing associations on whom their plan will place a burden if it is executed.

• Is the plan based on unsound ideas or inadequate knowledge? Here you must rally every academic you can get hold of. A great number of university disciplines will bear directly or indirectly on the plan: botany, ecology, geography, engineering, environmental studies, transport economics, sociology, mental health, architecture, agriculture and many others which may be represented among your members. They should have a field day with any of the facts, assumptions and influences that bear on their special subject: they can quote references and books and learned journals, some preferably in foreign languages, to prove that the plan springs from confused thinking and ignorance of the true facts, and is now fifteen years out of date.

6. The Attack on the Facts

For this attack you need a different section of your Experts' Cell: administrators, planners, top managers and staff officers from the services; if you have a statistician, you are really in luck. The skill you need is the skill of putting up lengthy proposals supported by convincing details. Only people who have actually done this have any real insight into the devices and dodges which buttress these shaky constructions and make them stand up. There are certain well-known weak points in all these documents which perhaps ought to be listed.

- The criteria. **Nearly all these plans list very early on certain criteria which any plan must fulfil. Miraculously**, **it turns out that this plan fulfils all of them**. **You are meant to think that the planners started from the criteria and eventually arrived at the plan**. **In fact**, **of course**, **it happened the other way round**. No good planner begins to formulate criteria until the plan is complete: he then evolves them by listing any plausible criteria which the plan can be shown to meet. Your answer is to challenge these criteria: (why does it have to be near the coast? Why is proximity to a motorway so important? Why does it have to be completed by 2002?) and at the same time suggest criteria the plan has omitted; not just 'minimum disruption of the existing community' (though why not?), but 'fitting in with all national and regional plans for the area,' 'based on latest knowledge and research' – any criteria, in fact, by which you can show the plan to be a failure.

- Hidden alternatives. 'There are two alternatives'; 'There are three possible approaches'; 'This can be solved in one of four ways.' Look at all these assertions very hard: they are nearly always an attempt to leap over a gap in the argument. A little reflection can usually turn up nine or ten additional alternatives and approaches, and one or two may be very interesting indeed.

- Evaluation of alternatives. It has been trouble enough for

Sir Humphrey to make the published plan appear to stand up, but in order to dissemble its arbitrary nature, he has to appear to consider alternatives. We saw in (ii) that there may be better alternatives, but it is also possible that his staff have actually considered some genuine alternatives: if, for instance, they were instructed to, or if a proposal has had wide publicity, or if an important faction wanted it. It is enormously tedious to argue right through several plans, and marvellous if some conclusive reason can be adduced for dismissing the others very early on. Examine the grounds for such dismissal very closely – they may well turn out to be much less solid than the plan suggests. If you can show that a good alternative has been wrongfully dismissed, you have opened a wide breach in the plan's defences.

- Factual accuracy. Do not expect all the facts to be accurate, and try checking up on any that look questionable. When the massive Beeching plan was published by British Rail a Cheshire schoolboy thought there was something funny about their figures for usage of the line behind his house. So he spent a day counting, and found the line enormously busier than the report said. On investigation it emerged that British Rail's survey had been conducted during the fortnight when the colliery that constantly used the line was closed for the summer holidays. Checking the facts of the plan would make an excellent project for a local school, and if you can call on any teachers (better still, head teachers) there is no reason why a small army of lively scrutineers should not find that sort of hidden treasure.

- New facts. Many of the report's facts may be based on out-of-date information – the 1981 census instead of the 1991, five-year-old government reports and projections. Even better, your colleagues attacking the concept may supply new material published after the plan was completed which disproves, say, the traffic growth trend on which the report is based. In particular it is worth checking the vintage of any facts or assumptions you feel have been around for a long time: even if nothing new has come to light, facts taken from a 1978 report lose a certain weight over the years.

- The unmentioned facts. **The planners will have suppressed a number of facts which damage their case. How can you find them? The best way is to go to all the sources which they have used for their information.** They may not willingly disclose them, but a sharp letter denying the accuracy of an assertion will usually elicit chapter and verse, and you can then get to work on other chapter and other verses for the less convenient facts. Once you have laid hands on these source documents, you have another excellent schools Civics project: 'How would you use the same source documents to rebut the plan which they are at present being used to support?' Sixth Forms, this time. **If you are opposing a retail development, get a retail expert to scrutinise the developer's figures. You will often find significant understatement of things like traffic congestion in local roads and loss of trade to the town centre.**

- Statistical selection. When a football writer tells you that a club has lost six out of its last seven home matches, that is a statistical selection: they have probably lost six out of their last twelve home games, or six out of their last twelve matches, but that is too ordinary to be worth reporting. So he selects seven as his base, and sticks to home matches. The plan is full of statistical selection: 'In the past ten years . . .' Why ten? Why not five, or fifteen? 'It has risen to 30 per cent since 1986.' Why 1986? Why not 1979? You need a trained statistician to do full justice to the plan, but anyone who is alert to the technique can expose a great deal of selective activity behind the scenes, particularly if he can get hold of a copy of that short and lively classic *How to Lie with Statistics* by Darrell Huff, to read.

- Selective deduction. Related to the hidden alternative. 'The low usage figure shows that there is too little public demand . . .' It may indeed. But it may show that the price is too high. Or that the public does not know about it. Or that it is so inefficiently run that people can't be bothered to wait for ages, and then finish up with something different from what they asked for.

- The architect's drawing. The great welter of plans, sections and elevations are meaningless to the councillors who are not in the building business. They will affect to give them serious study, but in fact their judgment will be entirely swayed by the architect's drawing. It will be the usual, idealized, fairyland picture – one car on the road, one in the car park, two girls in summer dresses, bright sunny day, trees in full leaf, exaggerated perspective, and the building bright and shining in all its glory. You cannot fight pictures with words, and it is simple today to draw a montage and place it over the original picture to show the true effect.

You must get an *architectus diaboli* to do an equally accurate architect's drawing with bare trees under a leaden sky during the rush hour, cars jamming the foreground, washing hanging out, with the paintwork starting to peel and the white stonework staining to grey in patches after a season or two of exposure to car exhaust, acid rain and fog. Yours is likely to be far more true to life – if you doubt it, contrast the architect's drawings of the National Theatre with the subsequent reality.

7. The Attack on the Figures

This is the third sub-division of the Experts' Cell, and for this you need people who understand the building business – architects, civil engineers, surveyors, contractors – as well as accountants, since you have to look behind the published figures.

One thing you can depend on: the plan will state that it is the cheapest plan by a factor of at least 20 per cent, and more likely 50 per cent. If there is not very much in it, there is a ghastly possibility that the planners will have to go back and do all the work again for the alternative plan. By demonstrating the overwhelming cheapness of their plan compared with all the others, they save themselves the labour and tedium of giving you or your elected representatives a choice, with all the consequent arguments and delays that make democracy so much less efficient than bureaucracy. This makes the attacks on the costs extremely important and also extremely promising: there is every chance of finding some highly questionable assumptions if you look carefully.

Your attack must be two-pronged: you have to show that the costings of the published plan are too low, and that the estimates for rival schemes are too high.

- Since the figures in the published plan will have to be worked to, if it is accepted, they are likely to be sound as far as they go. This is not to say you will not find optimistic understatements – you almost certainly will – but do not expect to find anything indefensible.

- Their published figures will be large sums under a few headings. You cannot attack successfully unless you make them convert these into smaller sums under many headings. You need someone who knows the business to list the headings – over a hundred, if possible – and you then ask them to fill in the detailed sums. If they comply, you can get to work: if they refuse, you can fill in your own estimate. You also have an invaluable piece of ammunition for later propaganda use – what are they trying to hide from you?

- There is more future in the omitted costs: most plans have repercussions which will also cost money, though not necessarily to the department which originated them: a motorway may entail strengthening the foundations of a church, moving a school may mean extra travel costs for a lot of families, and there is no guarantee that these costs will have been included.

- Cost-benefit may prove a good approach. What does the community gain from the plan and is it the best value for the money? A cost-benefit approach to the value of Ministry of Defence buildings in London showed that it would be cheaper to sell them all and billet the troops at Claridge's and the Dorchester. **You can always take the five million they propose to spend on the multi-storey car-park, and show what it could mean in terms of extra schools or hospital beds or anything else the community needs**.

- Community disruption and discomfort. The plan is unlikely to contain a full and vivid description of how the community will suffer from lorries, noise, loss of parking and play-space, and the other unpleasant consequences of the work when in progress, nor of what it will have permanently lost when the plan is complete. You should feature all these prominently, and put a cost to each one, and let the planners challenge the figures. They will then be in the position of having to say that an avenue of plane trees or the ability to park in the road by the shops is not all that important and this will in no way weaken your public support.

- It is when you turn to their costing of the alternative plans that you are likely to strike an even richer seam. Here too you should ask for a cost breakdown under a hundred or more separate headings. This will cause much annoyance, because they will not have gone into that sort of detail. If they refuse or delay, you can again write in your own figures, making sure they add up to less than the published plan: this will then make them provide details in self-defence, and give you valuable material to work on, or let their case go by default.

- They may well have ignored new techniques and materials which could considerably reduce the cost of alternatives, so your building expert should study these. Remember that the planners' ideal alternative route involves tunnelling through four and a half miles of solid granite, pierced every hundred yards by swift underground rivers. You may have to point out to them a simpler route or site that they have missed, and show them how it would reduce the costs.

- You may find in this part of the investigation that they are including categories of contingent cost that they have omitted from the costing of the published plan. This will be a valuable piece of ammunition later.

- Subject all their financial techniques to scrutiny. Ask for their discounted cash-flow projections. Ask what rate of

wages and materials–cost inflations they are assuming. Find out if they are expecting a rise in rate revenues. If you can show they have got their sums wrong on a plain accounting level, you are in a strong position.

8. The Alternative Plan

The Experts' Cell has one further responsibility, and it is a vital one. They have to prepare the alternative plan. As they examine and attack the published plan, they will build up a store of knowledge and a growing understanding that will qualify them to put forward a convincing alternative that either stops, moves, radically transforms or makes acceptable the plan you are objecting to. **The alternative plan is one of the pillars on which your case rests; it is extremely hard to fight a purely negative campaign. Whereas if you have a positive proposal the whole case takes on a new complexion.** The alternative plan will almost certainly be pooh-poohed by Sir Humphrey as impracticable or too expensive, because that is one of the conventions of the game: but so long as he cannot prove that it contains errors or betrays ignorance of the realities, your hopes of success begin to grow. A good Experts' Cell can usually make sure that the alternative plan is one that has to be debated, not just dismissed.

9. Publicity: The Strategy

As with your approach to influential organizations, the strategy is to start locally, and in a small way, and move wider and higher as you have more and more interest and support to show. But in general your aim is to get all the publicity you can, for the following reasons:

- The press, radio and television are instinctively on your side. You speak for the mass of people who buy their papers and watch and listen to their programmes, and you also save them from becoming passive recipients of official information. You are news and you are controversy, and they welcome you for it.
- Anyone seeking election by several thousand people depends for most of his votes on people who only know of him through the media, and it is very much in his interest that the pictures they see should be of a genial uncle distributing prizes at the school art exhibition, and not six people with swastika armbands giving him the fascist salute as he goes into the town hall.
- **Public officials are terrified of adverse publicity**: it is one of the few ways in which their errors and miscalculations can be exposed to the public and brought to the attention of very senior people on whom they may one day depend for promotion.

- Publicity for your cause will bring you supporters and alliances from surprising quarters, and the press cuttings will usefully substantiate your letters to influential bodies.
- Publicity is a stimulant drug which, when injected into your supporters' egos, will provoke bursts of redoubled energy.

To make full use of publicity, however, you need an understanding of public interest, public emotions and public reactions, as well as some insight into the mentality and motivations of the people who have to gauge public responses professionally. **It is of enormous value if the leader of your Publicity Cell can have had practical experience of journalism**, **advertising**, **public relations**, **television or radio**, **and it is even better if you can muster two or three more with those skills**. You should also try to recruit a good schoolteacher, not only because of the occasions when you may need a school's resources, but also for clear, direct and simple writing of English. Since part of this cell's work is to devise newsworthy forms of protest (parades, pageants, exhibitions etc.) you will need someone with a flair for invention and skill in theatrical production. In the absence of a professional, this is best solved if the teacher has experience of producing school plays. The other people you need in the cell, or closely connected with it, and those who can supply the technical skills and facilities you will have to call on: a photographer, a printer, a poster or lettering artist, a carpenter, a cartoonist.

Three basic essentials for a good campaign are a logo, a slogan and a song. A song needs to be born, or adapted, at a moment of high emotion: if someone starts up with 'We Shall Overcome' or 'We Shall Not Be Moved' at the first protest rally, it can become a campaign song. It is better still if someone has suitable simple words for a well-known tune like 'John Brown's Body' or 'When the Saints Go Marching In' to introduce at the emotional peak: but anything too novel, unmemorable or contrived, will fail.

The slogan has to be brief and simple – it must easily fit a banner. 'Hands off Pinner'; 'Save West Acton'; 'People – Yes! – Motorways – No!' Originality is not particularly important. The logo must be easy to draw, distinctive and easy to recognize – that of the Campaign for Nuclear Disarmament (CND) was excellent on all counts. You can always adopt an existing symbol that is well known in another context – the 'No Entry' sign, for example.

In dealing with the press, radio and television there are certain basic principles to follow:

- Your best ally is the editor of the local paper. If he is prepared to support your cause, that is excellent: but it is sufficient if he remains impartial, so long as he gives enough space to your campaign. Respect his editorial independence: do not put pressure on him (social or moral) to take your side or to suppress the other's case. He will be much more at ease with you if you do not put him on the defensive, and at ease over a drink, he may come up with any number of useful ideas and hints for wider publicity through his professional dealings with the national press and broadcasting.

- Build as close a relationship as you can with your local radio station or stations. They are chronically short of good local news, items and topics for local features, and in addition, they are always on the look-out for strong local issues for their innumerable and interminable phone-in programmes. And brief your members to find any opportunity they can to phone in themselves, to relate national topics like planning and environment to your specific case. Public officials and corporate bureaucrats hardly ever take part in phone-ins, so you are likely to have the audience to yourselves. On top of this, a friendly local radio reporter is another source of good advice about getting your case onto the national networks.

- Only in desperation should you think of wasting precious funds on newspaper advertising. The main news columns are not only free (so long as you are newsworthy), they are many times more effective in getting your cause across.

- Detail your best letter-writers to keep up an active campaign in the correspondence columns of the local press, and also to keep an eye open for relevant topics in national papers which reference to your case might illuminate. ('. . . interested to read Lord Gallstone's comments on confusion in Whitehall. We in Winterbourne Underwood, on a smaller scale, have had similar . . .)

- Always react. Reply to any critical letters, rebut any false allegations, correct errors of fact, expose misrepresentation, comment on new developments, challenge contrary views. The worst error in publicity policy is to say, 'We would do better to keep quiet.' Never let your cause go by default. And always reply instantly – in the case of daily papers, fax, telephone or e-mail it through, so that it appears in the issue immediately following the one it is replying to. If you do not, many people will look in that issue for your reply and, seeing it is not there, assume you have no answer.

- **Occasionally the press will come to you**, **but most of the time it is you who will have to take the initiative**. Before you make any approach, think of your cause from the newspapers' point of view; they do not want to repeat old arguments, dig up old events, or canvass old opinions. Your cause may live for you, but if you have nothing new to offer their readers it is dead for them. Moreover you will do yourself actual harm if you keep bombarding them with substantially unchanged material. You do not want to become one of those pestilential, boring groups of protesters who keep asking for free space to promote their cause.

- Following on from (vi), remember the peak-and-trough principle. **Your publicity initiatives should be brought together at the peak points**, **when there is some new turn of events**. You will already have noted fixed dates – public meetings, final objections, inquiries – and your publicity campaign should be built round those. You can make a few of your own as well – presentation of petitions, the summer exhibition, 'How to Destroy a Community', the autumn rally with floats, your experts' press conference – but do not crowd them too close together and do not let smaller demonstrations and other publicity initiatives dribble out in the troughs. Six events or facts may make a feature together when none of them would rate space separately.

- As in your letters to the press, always look out for opportunities to harness your campaign to events in the world outside. Not just the vast national bandwagons like ecology and environmental pollution and global warming, but anything in the news or in the public mind. If everyone is watching the repeats of 'Henry VIII' on television, have a ceremonial execution of the plan outside the Tower of London. Tie in with the Boat Show or the Motor Show or the Grand National or the Royal Academy Summer Exhibition. Plans involving demolition can be related to anniversaries of the Blitz.

- Your interests overlap with those of the press, but they are not identical. The bigger the row the better, as far as they are concerned, but your aims are more precise and limited. You may not want to antagonize, or directly criticize, particular individuals or groups, but for them it is all part of the fun. So warn everyone to react very care-fully to questions like, 'Would you say the council is being pig-headed?' unless you want 'THE PIG HEADED COUNCIL' – ACTION GROUP as the next morn-ing's headline. It can take months of patient diplomacy to repair the damage of a monosyllabic reply.

• The press is hungry for pictures, and you can greatly increase your coverage if you give them something worth photographing. Many of your pageants, parades and pro-test processions will be designed with this in mind, but someone in the cell should be thinking about pictorial possibilities all the time. A very un-newsworthy retailers' protest once achieved national news coverage for a pound or two, simply by having a dozen members parade in Enoch Powell masks. They took the extra step of parad-ing where they knew that photographers would be pre-sent – the opening of the Conservative Party Conference – and this too you should always be on the look-out for.

• Supply your own photographs too. If no news photo-grapher is free, it is possible that your own photograph will be considered, especially by the local paper. You have a better chance with before-and-after pictures – the avenue of trees before the council felled them, the Geor-gian houses before they were demolished – either in the extremities of your own case, or in other plans the min-istry or council is carrying out elsewhere.

• Get to know the practical constraints on the press and broadcasting, and particularly your local paper: the length and form in which they like material, their final press date, the times when they are short of news. Consult them before you fix the dates and times of your events. You do not want to miss out because your report arrives an hour after the paper has gone to the printers, or because your march coincides with the opening of the school science block by the Education Secretary.

- **Always supply journalists and broadcasters with a typed photocopy of the basic information you want them to have**: the reasons for your opposition, errors in the plan, numbers of signatures on the petition, other bodies that support you, results of the local opinion poll and so forth. They may have got it wrong, they may not have thought it important at the time; a glance at the sheet as they write may do a great deal of good. And express some of it as verbatim quotes.

- Keep a folder, and even a wall display as well, of every piece of press coverage you get. The more articles that appear in the press, the more seriously your case will be taken. The danger is that people will assume the plan is basically sound and sensible: the more press coverage you get, the better your chance of turning it into 'the controversial plan' in the public mind.

10. Publicity: The Tactics

All the above principles are general, and apply to all newspapers and broadcasters. What about approaches to specific papers or programmes? **One of the first rules is that you must not play favourites with news**: **if you have a genuine piece of news that everyone would like**, **make sure they all get it**; if it is national news, a telephone call to the Press Association will reach all papers at once through the agency tape. But if you are dealing not with hard news but 'optional' kinds of story that you would like printed to publicize your case, but which are not of obvious news importance, you can approach the particular paper or magazine that might be most interested. How do you know which?

- A sensitive understanding of the editorial policies and interests of all the press only comes with long experience, but most people can sense that the same story is unlikely to be successfully submitted both to *The Lady* and *Private Eye*. The best guide is probably your own internal one on journals you take regularly – 'This is the sort of thing *The Daily Mail* is always reporting . . .' But there are certain stereotype stories, or ingredients in stories, which have perennial appeal to broad sections of the media and it is as well to be aware of them. The chief difference is between the popular press and the quality press; the difference is only a difference of emphasis, and a strong enough story in any category will make them both, but it is worth separating them, since we are talking about marginal interest stories and it is on these that the different emphasis is significant.

POPULAR PRESS

- The little-old-lady syndrome. The plucky eighty-year-old widow who is going to be forced to leave her home after sixty years. Human pathos, loneliness, vulnerability, dignity, powerlessness.
- Cheesecake. Your banner has more chance of making the front page when carried by a bikini-clad model than by a fifty year-old chartered accountant in dark suit and steel-rimmed spectacles.
- Bureaucrats ride roughshod over ordinary people. Cold-hearted officials driving their plans through despite the sufferings of human beings and the resistance of the community.

- Official suppression. Important facts, documents and reports concealed by ministry or town hall because they would look silly, or be exposed as incompetent, if they were published. (This goes down well with quality papers as well.)
- Ruggedly independent citizens' stubborn, single-handed defiance of officialdom. The farmer who warns the ministry men off his land with a shotgun, the pensioner who surrounds his house with barbed wire and puts Crimean War cannon in the front garden.
- Community up in arms. Self-help citizens mobilize their resources. Mothers with small children besiege town hall.
- Celebrities. Gazza opens protest exhibition. Vera Duckworth says, 'They'd better not try this on Coronation Street.'

QUALITY PRESS

- Damage to historical or architectural monuments or places with historical associations. (Don't forget that nineteenth century industrial ruins or even twentieth century buildings can be claimed to have architectural importance).

- Loss of solitary, lonely places; empty hills, wild heathland, marshland, isolated villages.
- Pollution; chemical or biological damage to environment, danger from fumes, effluent and industrial waste.
- Ecology; upsetting the balance of nature, danger to wild animals or rare plant life.
- Antiquarian oddities of law: council's plans thwarted by statute of Edward III or the Long Parliament.
- Councillors insensitive to matters of the spirit or motivated by base desires for increased rate income or building work for their firm: Corruption. Nepotism. Freebies.

TELEVISION

Television, with its wide range of programmes, is liable to be interested in all these types of story, popular and quality. In addition, there are certain extras which give them an additional incentive. News, documentary and current-affairs producers send film cameras out to places like yours in order to vary the somewhat monotonous texture of studio items and to bring 'real life' to the screen. This is partly achieved by the place – out of doors instead of inside studio walls – and partly by the people. The people who dominate their programmes are conventionally dressed, articulate, educated, middle-class men and women, mostly between twenty-five and sixty, talking confidently and fluently about subjects that do not move them very deeply, within an agreeable, familiar and secure programme formula, where nothing disturbing, surprising or unexpected can ruffle the smooth predictability of the format. You will therefore be looked on with special favour if you can offer:

★

- Situations which develop in front of the camera, unrehearsed happenings where no one knows what is going to come next, interesting contests or trials of strength or attempts to set up new records: these have much more appeal than routine marches with banners.
- Wrinkled old faces, especially if they talk well and with regional accents.
- Eccentrics, in behaviour or dress or both.
- Confrontations, e.g. between the citizen and authority, which actually happen while the camera is there – farmers protesting about BSE policy to the Minister of Agriculture on his visit to the Bath and West Show, for example.
- Anyone who can talk with real passion and feeling.
- Enterprising children, especially the younger ones, and especially if they are showing creative skill: a school drama group enacting the protest march, the music group singing the protest song, the art class exhibition of 'our street.'
- Mothers with babies in arms/prams, toddlers.

All the media, but particularly television, react against the idea of being used as a publicity vehicle to promote other people's causes, so you need an objective news value before you approach them. They also react against people who are trying to muzzle them, and it is reputed that one group of protesters got excellent coverage through a member who used to ring the press and television the day before in a hectoring upper-class voice and tell them not to cover this exhibitionist display by a tiny handful of trouble-makers, that it would be irresponsible to publicize people who opposed the rightful authority, and that he would make trouble if they sent their cameras and reporters just because the other lot were covering it.

PART THREE

The Battle is Joined

I. The Start of the Campaign

So there you are. You have held your opening meeting, hundreds of people turned up, and it was a great success. The Action Committee was authorized to proceed, you all met, and went away to form your separate cells. Now you have formed them, varying in membership size from three to eight, and they have all been briefed on their objectives and their strategy. Now you have to put your strategy into effect.

The first step is the council of war, to which all cell-members should be invited: an attendance of less than thirty is unsatisfactory, and it should be over forty. No English reticence over identity – people must have lapel badges with their name and cell, and be given a list of every cell-member with address and brief biographical details: there is no time for this group to grow together gradually or casually, it must be pressure-welded. This meeting has to convert general emotion into unified and organized resolve, and there are certain points that have to be made when addressing it.

- Point out that the enemy were expecting reaction of shock, outrage and protest, and are now simply waiting for it to die down before proceeding as gradually and quietly as possible. The answer to this tactic is an organized campaign to ensure that the protest does not die down.
- Explain the organization, introduce each Action Committee member, and let him briefly explain what he sees as his cell's responsibilities, and the sort of help he needs

from other cells. (This may also lead to further recruits for his own cell being suggested by people who know of journalists, solicitors, surveyors, etc who have so far been missed.)

- Outline the shape of the campaign as you see it developing (see below) so that people realize the extent of the task and their own cells' likely peaks and troughs. Tell them all the fixed dates and events (objections, inquiries etc.) If you do not make it quite clear at this stage what people are letting themselves in for, you may suffer serious defections later on as the truth dawns.

- Make it clear that victory is eminently possible, if necessary by quoting previous successes: for example, Oxleaze Wood was saved, the original published route of the M4 motorway was moved in six places by the efforts of community action groups.

- After the outline speeches, invite maximum participation from everyone; not just questions, but ideas and information as well. It must come over clearly that this campaign is not being run by the Action Committee; the Committee is planning and steering, but the information, ideas and drive come from the cells.

After the council of war, you need another meeting of fifty or sixty people – the Action Committee plus all the street or district representatives. It will differ in detail and emphasis from the council of war, but it has the same purpose and should follow the same pattern. If each of fifty people can guarantee to bring a group of ten to any meeting or parade or demonstration, your whole campaign rests on a sound base.

2. The Shape of the Campaign

There is a sense in which the pattern of an old-fashioned campaign is very like that of an old-fashioned war: if the first assault is met successfully, there is a pause, then a second, bigger clash. If this too is inconclusive, there is an even longer pause followed by an even more prolonged engagement with both sides deploying all the resources they can mobilize. In your terms, it translates like this:

- The first assault. This was the publication of the plan, and you met it with your first public meeting.
- The first pause. Here you have to work fast behind the scenes. You must organize people – you have already started this with the cells. You must mobilize resources – the Funds Cell and the Grass-roots Cell are at work. You must look for allies. Above all, you must collect information about the enemy and start exploring possible terms of settlement. It may be that the whole thing can be averted now; unlikely, but worth taking soundings.
- Preparing the counter-attack. This, as we shall see, puts most weight on the Experts' and Publicity Cells. It includes a heavy barrage to soften up the enemy and weaken his resolve.
- The counter-attack. This will be your next real peak.
- The second pause. This is where you hope to end the campaign with a negotiated settlement. But you stay fully mobilized and defiant – quite apart from anything else, you weaken your negotiating position if you look anything less than enthusiastic to pursue the campaign to victory.
- Full mobilization. If you cannot negotiate a settlement, this is the crunch. It involves counsel and a public inquiry and television – everything you've got.

- The pitched battle. The full-scale public inquiry.
- The big powers. Whether you win or lose, all is not lost so long as your morale is high and you have strength and will to go on. Now you move into the world of ministries, political parties and the high councils of government
- The settlement. If this goes against you, only a change of minister, or government, can help you.

3. Pre-Emptive Diplomacy

You are now in the first pause, and the Headquarters Cell must get to work without delay. Their job is a diplomatic one and its details will be dictated by events, but there are certain immediate imperatives:

- They must find out who the real enemies are.
- They must quickly sort out potential allies on the council or in the ministry or the town hall, and also find which enemy supporters are only tepid and which are uncommitted.
- **They must discover where the real power lies. Is the chairman of the planning committee the real force, or is he the catspaw of the leader of the council, or a rubber stamp for the Chief Planning Officer? Always expect to find more real power behind formal authority if the man has held the job for a long time.**
- They must explore areas of disagreement about the plan. Do certain important people lack confidence in the costing, or question some of the figures, or suspect the growth forecasts?
- They must investigate the wider political situation with the enemy camp. Are there jealous factions within the

majority party? Are there rivals for jobs within it? Is there a running battle between the town planning department and the surveyor's department? This will mean a study of the political history of the council over the past few years, its rows and divisions and traumatic experiences. They should give particular study to any project that resembles the present one, since its proponents' tactics are likely to be much the same, modified by any painful lessons they have learnt.

• They must find good sources of information. This does not mean espionage (though some protesters are rumoured not to have recoiled from infiltration of offices and unauthorized perusal of documents) but it may mean cultivating the indiscreet, the unwary, and the poor dissemblers. Of course a complete run-down of the enemy plans is a valuable windfall, but that is the jam: the bread and butter is the gossip, the personalities, the news about promotions or reprimands or discontent or pressure that will help the negotiators to apply their leverage to the right places.

★

The more natural gossips you have in Headquarters the better: in conversation, pieces of information start to fit together, memories are jogged, new lines of inquiry are devised, and you begin to construct a solid information base for your next move. That is the diplomatic offensive, and it has five principal objectives:

- See if the plan can be defeated before it gets any further. It is unlikely, but it has to be explored. This entails a great deal of secret diplomacy – confidential conversations which cannot be quoted or referred to subsequently. Do not make the mistake of rushing off to parley with the chief enemy representatives: you may make awful blunders or miss glaring opportunities. Talk to the more friendlily disposed first, and find out the lie of the land. **See who your allies are**. **With a groundswell of support from councillors**, **a strong-looking legal case**, **and unenthusiastic officials**, **you may be able to go to the enemy in a position to negotiate terms at once**.

- Once you have established sources of information, start collecting it. An early settlement is extremely unlikely, and the other purpose of secret diplomacy is the gathering of information. Here too you succeed best by starting with friendlily disposed councillors, and moving on to the neutrals before you talk to the chief enemy. Is this the third draft of a plan that has been rejected twice, or is it brand new? Do any people believe in it passionately, or is it compliance with an instruction? Whose career will be damaged if it goes through? Who has the most private doubts? All these questions, all the information on the tensions behind the plan – administrative, political, personal – on the information and principles it is based on, on the hoped-for timing of its implementation, will arm you for your meetings with your real opponents and help you to gauge more accurately the disposition of their defences and the most promising lines of attack for the future. Are they sure of their political support? Do they feel they can depend on the ministry to back them up? How sound is the engineering thinking behind the plan? Little nuances here and there can save a lot of wasteful attacks on strong positions – but only if you go into the meeting with good background knowledge. And remember that they are looking for indications as to where your line of attack will develop, so keep your disclosures to a minimum.

- Obviously you will gather all the political support you can, but it may not be very much. We have already seen that it will be fatal to make this a party issue, certainly at this stage, and you should not expect too many people to support you before the counter-attack. This does not apply to lower-level authorities: you may well get the parish council's support against the county council, or even the county council's support against the ministry, but the lower-level authority's support will get you nowhere against united and resolute opposition at a higher level.

  Your MP is a valuable ally at this stage. It is difficult to get him to come out against the plan unless it is a huge ministry one which is being opposed by the council as well; **but a good constituency MP can be of great use simply by helping to see that you get fair treatment**. **If you can**, **get him to raise a question in Parliament that will have everyone in the ministry scurrying around for days**; and although the Parliamentary Commissioner is not the Ombudsman some people once hoped for, he can be a thorn in the flesh of a department, and the only way to him is through your MP. Your MP should also be a fund of sound practical advice on tactics and relations with the press.

- Your objective is to keep the enemy's unity and resolution to a minimum until you have the chance to demonstrate yours. Your hope is that when they see your counter-attack they will have second thoughts, but second thoughts are hard to admit if you have already nailed your first thoughts to the mast.

You therefore have to start sowing the suspicion that this may be another Stansted, and that much is to be gained by waiting. The speech you do not want made when the plan is debated by the council is, '. . . an excellent plan which we shall be proud to see take shape. Let us now press forward, despite the disruptions of a handful of trouble-makers blinkered by their narrow interests, and brook no delay . . .' What you want is, '. . . an excellent plan, on which we must congratulate the committee and the department for their tireless labours. Let us now lay it before the wider community and show that our administrative skill is matched by our democratic instincts, so that if and when it is accepted it will truly be the people's plan, and not something imposed on them by planners. I cannot reveal that such scrutiny will reveal any flaws – but if it does I cannot believe that we shall regret having them exposed before we commit ourselves to the labour and expense . . .' Between these two speeches – both favourable to the plan – lies the difference between defeat and victory. You must work for the maximum number of speeches couched in the vein of the second rather than the first, and for the maximum number of people keeping open their option to join you later.

- **Do not seek personal glory**. If you create a situation where the defeat of the plan means everyone climbing down and admitting that you were right and they were wrong, you have landed yourself with a battle to the death. **At this stage**, **give other people the chance to**

gain credit by sponsoring your cause, **not merely to lose it by opposing you**. So your use of the press should be highly conciliatory at this stage. '... very sensible speech by Councillor Niggle. We are delighted to see that the council are not rushing headlong into the plan.'; '... most reassuring interview with Alderman Pompworthy. In some local authorities, this plan would already be a *fait accompli*, and be jackbooted through. Thank heavens our council has more democratic instincts – people are keeping their minds open till we all know a bit more ...'; '... found the Chief Planning Officer's attitude very proper. As he says, his job is to prepare the best practicable plan within the terms of reference, not to tell the community what's good for it. And if practicability changes or the terms of reference were inadequate he is certainly not to blame.' You can also comb their election speeches for pompous platitudes in service of your cause: 'As Councillor Woodnutt said last May, "It's the people who matter, and the quality of life that each and every one of us has a right to enjoy." That is precisely what this issue is about – people and the quality of life. I'm sure a man like Councillor Woodnutt won't go back on his word now.' The more people who feel they can actually enhance their reputations by opposing the plan, the better you have done your work.

The only exception to this is the councillor with a genius for getting all the other councillors' backs up, especially in his own party. Most councils have one of these. If you can arrange for the plan's implementation to be the cause he harnesses his case to, that is quite acceptable.

- Your final objective in this phase is to collect ammunition for later use. Whereas information is collected by secret diplomacy, ammunition is collected by open diplomacy –

correspondence and formal, minuted meetings. The purpose of this sort of diplomacy is to build a file of material you may want to use later, and meetings take place chiefly in order to generate minutes or confirmatory letters. You must make sure that everything you want to establish gets onto paper. This may be undertakings: 'Thank you for your assurance that there will be proper advance consultation with those affected . . .'; 'Glad to know your minds are still open . . .' Or it may be admissions: 'Councillor Gross said he was not acquainted with the North-West regional plan at the time of his original speech'; 'The council refused to disclose the source of the figures in paragraph 41. . .' **Even if they take minutes, you should do so too,** '**for our own records**' **since minutes, although masquerading as dispassionate summaries of conversations, are in fact manacles for shackling men to their words**. In the hands of a skilled minute-taker (and you may well find you have one – the Civil Service are streets ahead of the field, with the Treasury and FO up at the front) they are masterpieces of discreet selection and subtle phrasing. There is a world of practical difference between 'undertook to inform residents' and 'undertook to inform residents wherever possible' – the difference between 'said he would' and 'said he would not' – and there are devices like producing enormously long minutes in longhand and sending off a bad photocopy if you want to slip through an admission they made but might retract if they saw it on paper; and never putting that sort of admission within six lines of the recipient's name or post, since his eye will stop at each of those during even the most hasty perusal.

- **Some of your supporters may urge direct action in contravention of the law**: **digging up roads, camping in trees, sabotaging vehicles, stealing equip-**

ment. Quite apart from any moral considerations, which might not deter them, there are three practical reasons why this is an extremely bad idea.

(a) It cannot work. Every authority knows that if it allows its decisions to be overthrown by violent action, it will be opening the floodgates. It is the same argument as with hi-jackers and hostage takers; to give in is to broadcast the fact that if people are extreme enough you will back down.

(b) Illegal protests act as a magnet for people outside the area who enjoy a punch-up with the police and are more interested in highly publicised confrontations with authority than in advancing your cause.

(c) A stand-off between protestors and the bailiffs and bulldozers will certainly grab media attention, and the focus is likely to be on the behaviour of your more extreme allies. As a result your public reputation as law-breakers will turn a lot of moderate people against you – people whose support you are going to need. This puts a powerful weapon in the hands of your opponents.

4. The Barrage

The barrage is chiefly a paper barrage, and most of this section is devoted to the loading, aiming and firing of letters; but you will also have to use the telephone from time to time. You will do well to think of the telephone simply as a means of acquiring information; it is not as good as a letter for conducting arguments, extracting admissions or making representations, except in emergencies – for instance when you see through the window that the bulldozer driver is actually fastening the chain round the oak tree that is under a Tree Preservation Order.

Most of your work will be done through junior officials at lower levels. There are two points to watch:

- Always take the full name of the person you are talking to, and make sure they know you are writing it down ('. . . just a moment, Mr Phillips, that's two l's and one p, is it? And Antony with or without the h?') This means that they will actually pass on the message, actually find out the answer, actually ring you back, three or four times more expeditiously and reliably than if you let them ring off without stripping away the cloak of secure bureaucratic anonymity.

- Always be polite to junior staff, and get on the friendliest telephone terms you can. It is not just that they can, if they have a mind, do you more harm than you think; there is a positive side to it as well. In your jokey conversations and happy laughing chats all sorts of little clues and nuances will slip out which will be suppressed if your offensive hectoring imposes a terse and toneless formality in your respondent. **And the more widespread the feeling in the town hall or the ministry that you are really jolly nice and reasonable people with a genuine grievance and a genuine case**, **the better your chances**. If the office consensus is that you are a vicious and unscrupulous pressure group, you will only strengthen their collective determination not to let you get away with it.

If you do find yourself talking to senior officials on the telephone, the question of tape-recording the conversations may arise. Should you or shouldn't you? This is a difficult question because there is not much precedent, but there are guidelines.

★

- Why are you doing it? If it is for later use as evidence at an inquiry, a letter is far more use. Tapes have been allowed in law courts, but so far only in the sort of case (e.g. corruption) where it is manifestly impossible to produce a better record. It would be difficult to get them admitted in a public inquiry.
- Do you tell your respondent that you are recording his replies? If you do, he is perfectly justified in saying that if you want a record you can write to him, and then ringing off. If you do not tell him, then even if you have no moral objection to deceit yourself you are likely to lose more than you gain amongst the people who have – and they are likely to be influential people. And once the news leaks out, you will probably find that everyone is instructed to refuse to speak to you on the telephone in any circumstance. You will have to write or call.
- The one use that is possibly defensible is when you simply want to listen again to an important conversation, either privately or with the members of your cell, to pick up significant facts or omissions or intonations. But again if the news gets around, or if you are tempted to give the recording a wider distribution as an object lesson in official arrogance or duplicity, you will probably face a telephone embargo.

But it is letters, not telephone calls, that carry the weight of the barrage. A large part of the campaign will be won or lost on paper, which is the chosen weapon of civilized government, and you can turn this to your advantage. A part of your objective has already been mentioned in the previous paragraph – the extraction of information and admissions which will be valuable to you later. The Experts' cell must put in all the work they can, and they may be surprised by the discrepancies they reveal when they compare replies from different departments and branches of government. The replies may also give them useful leads by betraying homework not properly done before the plan was published. A really wide spread of correspondence will be a great help when mounting the counter-attack.

But there is another purpose in the barrage. **A steady stream of sensible and critical letters that demand careful replies has a powerful softening-up effect**. **Officials will begin to realize that it is going to be a very tough campaign**, **giving them a lot of extra work and plenty of opportunities for slipping up or getting caught out**. After all, they have plenty of work to do, without answering tricky correspondence, and if every member of the Experts' cell is writing two or three letters a week, the cumulative effect after a month will be noticeable.

Whatever other economies you have to make, do not economize on your writing paper. Of course you can use what you like to order leaflets from the printer, but when addressing officials, the media, politicians or influential allies make sure you address them on best-quality paper with an embossed letterhead. It is worth every penny ten times over: it gives an aura of substance and authority to your representations, and an impression (however illusory) that there are funds and social status behind you; it warns potential enemies to think hard before they force issues, and encourages potential allies to feel that you are a far from hopeless cause. And although the word 'campaign' is frequently used in this report, be very wary of employing it on your letterhead. It suggests that you are an aggressor; words like 'defence' and 'resistance' express your cause more accurately and will serve it better.

The worst sort of letter, **from your point of view**, **is one that takes you an hour to compose**, **and is answered in two minutes**. **Conversely**, **the letter that**

you can dash off quickly, **and that keeps the official busy for a long time concocting the answer**, **is what you are aiming for**. His standard response to a letter from the public is to be brief, non-committal and uninformative. If he can simply reply, '. . . will bear your views in mind . . .', or '. . . ensure that your remarks be brought to the attention of . . .', or '. . . information not at present available . . .', then he has won and you have lost. If you have an experienced and senior civil servant in one of your teams, he should look at all the early letters and show the writers how they could have been improved, but the principle is straightforward enough: make sure your letter contains some suggestion that cannot be left unrefuted on the file. There are seven main categories of allegation or implication which sting them into activity.

• Ignorance: if they have to admit you know more than they do, their credibility in defence of the plan will be seriously eroded. So you can keep them busy with questions like, 'Surely section 43 para vi of the plan conflicts with the principles stated in Mr Tashima's famous paper at the Los Angeles environmental conference last April?' (A refinement is to give the wrong reference first time, so when they finally come up with that discovery you can say, 'I meant of course Mr Onishi's paper at Geneva – but surely you must have realized that from the context?') You can also play on this by disingenuous questions if they persistently block requests for facts; '. . . sorry you could not tell me the figures for 1989-90, but it does not matter as I have now found them in the 1991 report. Your answer shows that you cannot have read the report, which indeed is obvious from some of the false assumptions in the introduction to the plan . . .'

• Inconsistency: 'This is not the reason that Councillor

Forthright gave at the original meeting in the town hall.' 'This is in conflict with ministry circular 133/67.' 'You did not enforce this in 1994 in an identical instance.' Do not, of course, state what the circular or the councillor said – let them sweat.

- Inefficiency: '. . . when your representative arrived it transpired that no one had told him the subject of the meeting . . .'; '. . . now appears that you were in the building all the time, while we were being sent away because you . . .'; '. . . since you appear to have lost the minutes, I enclose or copy.'

- Favouritism, especially of influential people: '. . . cannot of course expect the privileges you extend to Sir William by asking you to visit us instead of our waiting your pleasure . . .'; '. . . quite understand that property as expensive as that in The Grove must receive special attention from your staff; nevertheless we too pay council tax, even if not in the same band . . .'; '. . . now find from Lord Cartridge that all his letters have been answered by return of post, while mine have taken between nine and twenty-two days . . .'

- Trespassing on politicians' territory: '. . . policy you speak of is certainly not the council's – this was made clear at Thursday's meeting with Councillor Brick. If the staff in the planning office have decided amongst themselves how the borough shall be developed, when may we expect the electors to be informed?'

- Trespassing on other departments' territory. This can be encouraged by judicious timing: '. . . glad to know that arrangements are being made for schooling to continue during Stage 11. Perhaps you could inform the Education Department of this, since their letter of the same date as yours says "no discussions have taken place as yet"'. It can also be helpful to your cause to circulate copies of your letters: '. . . very happy to accept your explanation on the telephone this morning that it was the ministry and not you who had slipped up . . .' (copy to ministry).

- Bureaucratic arrogance: '. . . of course appreciate (and perhaps you will permit me to add that your manner on the telephone makes it clear) that you are a busy and important man, and ordinary members of the public are a nuisance. But do please realize that our homes, even if they are much less imposing than yours in The Avenue, matter desperately to us . . .'

It is frequently a good technique to keep a shot in your locker. Your initial letter on any topic will draw their fire, but it will also make them unmask their batteries. So keep back one important fact for your second letter: '. . . in reply to your point that I should have ascertained the details from the Borough Surveyors' office, that is precisely what I tried to do. I called there on May 13th, and was told by Mr Clam that the facts were not to be made available to the general public.'

One of the standard bureaucratic responses is simply not to reply unless prodded, or to delay replying for a long time to gain breathing space, rather like lobbing in lawn tennis. You therefore have to stand at the net and smash, always replying by return, or else force them up to the net by the epistolary equivalent of a drop-shot, something that makes them move like lightning in order to save the point. To achieve this it is important to conduct your correspondence with the top man, even though his subordinates are replying on his behalf. There is a special reason for this: if you score a valuable point in correspondence with a subordinate official, the top man can always say, 'Your case has only just been brought to my notice. I am sorry about the confusion – there seems to have been a slip-up somewhere.' (Public officials sell their subordinates down the river more readily than any but the very largest business corporations.) He cannot say this if the reply will be, 'I am surprised the case has only just been brought to your notice, since it was to you I addressed the letter.' – and his subordinate will treat your letter that much more carefully for knowing that the reply carries his boss's reputation as well as his own.

Always use the top man's actual name. **You will do much better to address the Permanent Secretary as 'Dear Sir Humphrey'**. If you do not know it, find it out from one of the switchboard operators. And if he is eminent enough, look him up in *Who's Who*: you may find hidden treasure. He may be a vice-chairman of the National Trust, he may list walking as a hobby, he may have a botany degree – there could easily be some detail you can connect with your cause and work into your letter in such a way that he replies to you himself. Even if he passes it down, the use of his name and biographical details will ensure a respectful treatment from those who work under him.

You can also prod procrastinating bureaucrats by invoking an authority from a higher level. When dealing with the town hall a letter to the minister responsible for local government simply listing the delays (there need to be two or three at least of ten days to a fortnight) will elicit a neutral reply: '. . . sorry for the delay, but must ask you to be patient since our local government officers are understaffed and overworked . . .' The correspondence will nevertheless be sent down to the department, and it is a law of correspondence as of gravity that the greater the height from which a letter descends, the greater the force with which it hits the target. They will not want another such letter in a month's time. Another ploy is to write to Buckingham Palace. The Queen's staff cannot of course do more than pass your letter on to the appropriate department of government; nevertheless the fact of its having come from the Palace gives it a certain magical quality which should ensure swifter replies in the future. **There is scarcely a public official in this country over the age of forty whose mind does not from time to time revolve around the possibility of an appearance in an Honours List**, and what is more he knows very little about how the system operates in practice. Will his name be entered in the Royal Black Book if there are three complaints about his actions within twelve months? Will a frown darken the royal brow when the name of the Deputy Chief Planning Officer for North Wessex crops up over cocktails at Sandringham? It may be wildly unlikely, but then a couple of lines on the map changing the route of the pylons is a small premium if it will insure him against such an awful possibility.

You may also want to exploit the fact that distinguished people in public life are personally known by far more people than they can actually put a name or face to. What is more, very few of them – and no politicians – are willing to admit this sort of ignorance. So if you address one of the great and good as 'Dear Quentin' or 'Dear Elspeth' and sign with your own Christian as well as surname, the odds are tremendously in favour of your receiving a reply ' Dear Bill' or 'Dear Liz'. When this correspondence is circulated, the recipients in the Town Hall or Whitehall will hear alarm bells ringing and give special care and attention to their reply.

All the correspondence with officials comes under the heading of light artillery; you also have some heavy artillery at your disposal. Now is the time for the Influential Allies Cell to train the big guns on the enemy position, the bigwigs of the district and the significant national associations, societies and public bodies. They should all be briefed to ask for information and assurance and generally keep up the barrage, though you do not want them to come out publicly until the counter-attack: their objections should be in letters to you, for you to disclose at the right moment.

5. The Confrontation

The confrontation takes place at the mass meeting to which you invite the leading proponent of the plan to answer your questions, in person if possible, but if not then through a representative. Make the invitation a long time in advance, so that he cannot plead another engagement without looking transparently evasive. If he won't come and meet you, make him say so. If he is shrewd and experienced, it is possible that he will in fact hold this meeting himself and invite local residents. This is not so good for your cause, since it gives him the initiative and the appearance of democratic behaviour, and you cannot boycott the meeting without damaging your cause. ('If they are so concerned, why did they not come to the Chief Planning Officer's public meeting in the town hall?') Much better if you control the content and progress of the meeting, and he is in the position of a defendant summoned to answer charges. **Some more sophisticated planning applicants or officers are now not merely holding meetings but mounting exhibitions with plans, models, drawings and photographs. This should be countered by an alternative exhibition showing your interpretation of their proposal**.

Whichever way it happens the tactics are much the same. His intention is to commit himself to nothing, to keep the emotional tone low, to talk on the assumption that the plan is already agreed, to concentrate the discussion on small practical details, and to emerge as a sensible, reasonable fellow citizen who has done the best possible job in the circumstances, leaving everyone thinking that the human disruption and sacrifice are a pity but necessary for the greater good of the wider community. If the meeting is on his own ground, he will have the advantage of talking first and for some time about the details of the plan and of leaving a very short space for questions. He may even bring a dozen assistants and dissolve the meeting when he has finished talking, saying that they will all now answer individual questions. If he tries this you must jump up and object, saying there are many questions you all want to hear him answer publicly. In either case your basic tactics are the same:

- To keep the high emotional tone, by making sure you get a large meeting of supporters. This is not to shout the speaker down, but to react powerfully with cheers and applause to good points, or outbursts of protest at duplicity, evasion or unacceptable assertions.
- To avoid practical details and to keep to the question 'Will the plan happen or not?' instead of 'How will the plan work in practice?'

- To use questions not as a means of eliciting information but as weapons to inflict damage.

You will therefore need a maximum attendance of experts at this meeting, and a good discussion first to decide who are to ask what questions in what order. The order is important to force him into explicit assertions early on ('. . . certainly not vague and sketchy costings. We have gone extremely thoroughly . . .'), if you have a scoring point to make later ('You said just now the costings were extremely thorough. How then do you explain . . .?') The first question has deprived him of the reply, 'These costings are of course provisional . . .' You will also find that he is an expert at evading questions, so you must be on the look-out for this technique and expose it by shouting 'Answer the question!' – in unison if necessary – until you get an answer. Evasion is a weapon which you can turn back on the user by exposing it. You must also expect each question to be a question-sequence, since the questioner's real success is more likely to come by attacking the answer to his first question, and if he is successful he will need a final pseudo-question to drive his success home. ('So you admit that no one bothered to ask?' 'In other words you haven't kept up with the latest developments?' 'So in fact it could be done at half the price?') This should be understood in advance to prevent another questioner from cutting in and spoiling the *coup de grace*. You may know you have won, but the press who are reporting the meeting may need to have it underlined, and anyway, a good succinct line at the end gives you a better chance of a cheer or a round of applause.

There are six areas of attack for your questions, and the experts should have been working on the first three already. These should be the questions asked first, since they are the more intellectual and particular, though a real exposure of incompetence or duplicity will probably provoke an outburst. The last three are emotional and general.

- Quality of thinking: the basic concept – is there any need for the plan at all?
- Errors in the plan's facts or figures.
- Ignorance of books, papers, reports, articles, etc., which have a bearing on the plan.
- Lack of personal commitment. Who really stands by this plan? 'I put it to you that you have underestimated the costs by 50 per cent in order to get this plan through.' 'Nonsense.' 'Good, will you now undertake to resign if the final costs are 50 per cent above your estimate?' Any answer except 'Yes!' (which is highly unlikely) should get a hoot of laughter and leave no more to be said.
- Lack of general credibility. Go through past plans and compare them with what actually happened. (Concorde, for example, which cost 1,000 million pounds, was estimated as 135 million; the mid sixties air traffic projections for 1974 were clearly wild over-estimates and were moved to the 1980's.) Then bring up these discrepancies between plan and performance to undermine confidence in the whole planning business. ('Three years you said this scheme will take? Do you remember this plan of yours in 1983? That said three years, too; a new library and swimming bath in three years. Have you been to the site recently?'
- Lack of common humanity. 'Could you just describe to us how you think it feels to be turned out of the house you've lived in for seventy years?' 'You've gone into lots of costing details. What cost do you put on moving a handicapped child who has just settled down and made friends in a school for the first time? What cost do you put on a bedridden pensioner whose life revolves round visits from

the caring neighbours who you're going to take away? Come on, give us some figures: Ten pounds? Ten thousand pounds? Or don't you think about that sort of thing?' By all means quote actual cases of people in the audience.

The meeting (whoever has convened it) should end with a rousing statement of determination to resist, followed by prolonged cheers and perhaps the singing of the song. On a more sober note, someone should have been taking as full a report as possible of any statement, admission, evasion, commitment or refusal to answer that may be of value during the counter-attack. The audience should go home more than ever convinced of the rightness of their cause, the weakness in the enemy case, and of the possibility of victory: the enemy representatives should go off revolving in their minds the alternative plans if this one fails to get through.

PART FOUR

The Counter-Attack

The confrontation meeting was one of your peaks, and it will be followed by a trough. The trough this time, however, must be only a short one, because impetus is important at this juncture. So gear your cells up for the twin peaks of the counter-attack; the demonstration and the press conference.

I. The Objective

The objective of the counter-attack is simple: to stop the plan from happening. This does not mean that the other side will lay down their arms and surrender on the spot, only that the climate will be so changed after you have finished that a new committee will be set up, or some other form of quiet postponement will be devised, which allows the plan to die off slowly and quietly without anybody noticing.

If this is to happen, both the politicians (mostly still uncommitted if you have done your work) and the officials must be given a shock. The politicians must suddenly realize the extent of public unpopularity they may face if they press on, and the officials must see a real danger of ignominious defeat, or at best an enormous amount of work to defend the plan against an intensity of public scrutiny that it was not designed to withstand.

None of this will come about without publicity. Your aim, therefore, is maximum press coverage, national if possible, but if not then local and regional, on a large scale. **It is when councillors and officials start to see themselves through the eyes of the press and television that they will begin to think again**. So although your counter-attack will draw on all the cells for support, the Publicity Cell will be the spearhead.

2. The Petition

There are essentially two types of petition: one aimed at the local council and the other a Parliamentary Petition. The local one is fairly easy to produce. It just need a clear and brief statement of the course and its objectives as its heading. A Parliamentary Petition must adhere to a strict format, available from the House of Commons. Your MP is probably the best person to do this for you. It has to be clear and precise, with a full statement on the first sheet and an abbreviated header on each continuation sheet.

A petition has a number of beneficial side-effects, quite apart from its value as evidence of public opposition.

- It creates vigorous grass-roots activity and involves a great many people: it brings your case literally to everyone's doorstep.
- Petition collectors can canvass other support at the same time – 'Do try to come to the rally outside the town hall on Saturday: half-past two.' They can also pass on chosen pieces of information – 'Did you know that for the same price as this plan we could have a swimming bath, four nursery schools and sheltered housing for ninety people?'
- They can do a little bit of amateur polling: 'Would you support a candidate for the council if he promised to vote against the plan? Whatever his party?'

A petition has very little publicity value unless it attracts a good number of signatures, so the Grass-Roots Cell should set targets and run competitions between groups of petitioners and give individual mention in the newsletter to people who have collected 100, 250, 500 and so on. The intervals between citation numbers should be big enough to give a sense of achievement, but small enough to be within most people's reach. There are three points to brief petitioners on:

- The signatures may be needed for display, so collect them on loose-leaf sheets and on only one side of the paper. A single exercise book is much less impressive than sixty-four A4 sized sheets pinned to the wall.
- People don't like being the only signature, so never offer them a blank sheet. When starting a new page, present the previous completed page beside it.
- **It is absurdly easy to fake petitions – forgery, multiple signatures, etc. – and evidence of only one or two instances will invalidate the whole petition. Petitioners must therefore be scrupulously honest**, and every potential signatory must be asked if they have signed already (and not be allowed to sign again if they have!) The best way to avoid duplication is to complete the petition quickly. In Bristol, at the Golden Hill battle of 1992, 16,640 signatures were collected on a Parliamentary Petition in one week. It was then presented in the House of Commons by three MPs, one from each of the main parties.

3. The Demonstration

The purpose of the demonstration is to get itself into the newspapers and on to television. The larger your turnout, the more the media will feel this is a genuine local protest and not a stunt by a few self-publicists, so press for the maximum possible numbers.

However, readers and viewers have by now seen endless parades of people carrying banners so you must try and provide something more, something both visual and original, that will attract editors enough to commit their cameras to your event, and provide good enough pictures to gain you plenty of newspaper space and screen time. Some examples of the kind of idea that have this ingredient:

- Lady Godiva. Miss Hartley Wintney 1996 will ride naked through the streets at 3 p.m. on Saturday in protest against the plan, and all citizens are put on their honour not to look. This has the double merit of attracting press attention ('The Peeping Toms of Hartley Wintney ...' etc.) when announced, and further press attention when the council refuse permission,. You then have more ammunition for quotes: 'Samantha was only going to be there for ten minutes – the muti-storey car-park will be there all our lives.' 'What sort of council is it that spends two million pounds on a vast concrete eyesore and forbids people to look at a beautiful girl?' 'It's the car park that's going to be the affront to public decency, not Samantha,' etc., etc.
- The Mayor can't get into his car for red tape. 300 yards of red tape festoon his car when he comes out of the civic reception. It is easily removed – the point is not to stop him driving, but to get the colour photo of him gazing at it. As with Lady Godiva, you want to get readers and

viewers laughing at the enemy with you, not sympathizing with him.

- 'They treat us like a lot of sheep.' 200 sheep released in the town hall car park at 5 p.m. on Friday, as the officials leave work.
- If the council are cutting down trees try a Birnam Wood Parade: a thousand people carrying branches and greenery make a human wood in the town square – a forest of protest.
- The Juggernaut. Let the junior forms of the schools build lots and lots of houses from grocers' cardboard boxes, and bring them all together into streets and shops and squares: then hire or borrow a steam roller to enact the part of the council and squash them all flat while the brass band plays 'Colonel Bogey'. Finish up with a monster model of the town hall, which is smashed to tumultuous applause.

Any of these or similar demonstrations can culminate in the presenting of the petition. And to reiterate, the rule for demonstrations is that they should be original, visual (moving rather than static tableau-type), good-humoured, aiming at ridicule, massively well-attended, and containing some of the special ingredients that commend themselves to press and television (see Part 2, section 10).

4. The Press Conference

A press conference may sound too ambitious and may well be so – the editor of your local paper will advise you. But you have little to lose except effort, and a great deal to win. But remember that the press are not interested in giving you publicity: they want authentic new information of interest to their readers, and if you are to hold a press conference you must ensure that they get it. You are not asking for the top-line reporters to come down in strength: the news–gathering network is highly efficient, and wherever you live the chances are that every national paper and radio network will have a stringer, within easy reach. If your announce-ment/invitation makes it clear that genuine new facts will be released, it is quite likely that the editor will send a stringer on the off-chance.

Your letter is important. Do not send a duplicated circu-lar. There are probably no more than twenty newspapers, TV and radio stations you want to be represented, so find the name of each editor, and address him by name. (Do not put 'personal' on the envelope as this is a familiar and ir-ritating dodge which will turn against you. 'Personal' means it is a personal friend writing on a personal matter.) It is best if a regular reader writes each letter, so you may have to spread the work out beyond the publicity cell; editors are human, and if the letter refers with appreciation and detailed quotation to similar reports or features in past editions ('. . . know how effectively you expose bureaucratic oppression

... excellent report on the Tamar power station proposal ... your very good point in the leading article about the difference between real consultation and pseudo-consultation ... interesting new tactics in our case ...') its chances of a favourable hearing will not be diminished.

If you have any fears that only one or two of the press may turn up, and that the consequent humiliation may give heart to the enemy, you do not have to call the occasion a press conference. Instead, you can hold an exhibition, and simply invite the press as well as the rest of the local community. Even if you do call it a press conference, it is not at all a bad idea to hold the exhibition as well and conduct the conference in the exhibition room. The exhibition can be as ambitious as you like, with computer models, relief maps and oil paintings, but basically it can consist of quite simple wall displays. A designer or art teacher will be able to make it arresting and attractive. Possible ingredients include:

• Photographs (get the local photographic club to help):

> Past events in your campaign
> Petitioners at work
> People specially affected (pensioners in doorways, etc.)
> The threatened area
> The alternative areas
> Past monstrosities by the same authority
> 'Before' and 'After' photographs of previous projects
> Architects' drawing of previous project contrasted
> with photographs of the reality.

• Quotations specially lettered from:

> Ministers', MPs' or councillors' speeches
> Literature (Abraham Lincoln, John Stuart Mill on
> Liberty, etc.)
> Government documents

- Actual letters (or photocopies):

  Good ones from you
  Contradictory ones from authorities
  Climb-downs or hectoring letters from Sir Humphrey
  Letters of support from important people or public
      organizations

- Drawings

  Planners' drawing
  Architectus diaboli drawing
  Sketch-club drawings of what you are trying to
      preserve from destruction. School paintings of 'our
      town/borough/village'

- Press cuttings
- The petition signatures

All this material, quite apart from its local interest, has a chance of sparking off ideas in the minds of reporters: and the greater the variety of information, the more they will feel that they can write a different story from the others.

A few points of general guidance for conducting the press conference:

- Keep your address brief and factual. Don't try to convert the press. Put your case to them as information, not as evangelism, so that they can know what it is.
- This is the time your experts reveal all the holes they have picked in concept, costs, facts, logic, projections, statistics, to show that it is a shoddy plan and an unnecessary plan.
- Now, too, you reveal all the high-powered support you have gathered and show that the plan is anti-social and unpopular.
- Then you reveal alternatives. Although you will be going

nap on one of them later, it may be better at this stage to indicate several so that the enemy are kept in doubt. This should show that theirs is not even the best plan.

- Give plenty of time for questions after your address, and have all necessary experts on hand to answer them.
- Give time for private questions afterwards, and make sure all your people have lapel badges (the press should be given them too).
- When you hand out the lapel badges, give the press a sheet or two of information – all the facts you want them to have – and any photographs you can afford.
- Expect critical questions, the sort the enemy would put, and do not resent them. The press want to know how you answer the other side's case, and they will treat them in the same way.
- Try and think of any people the press might want to interview, make sure these people are available, and make sure the press know it.

Throughout the whole period of the counter-attack, and especially at the press conference, avoid criticism of anyone who has not publicly and irrevocably committed themselves to the enemy cause. Your new information is one of the best weapons for this if correctly used ('. . . when he said that, he did not of course know . . .'), and the fewer your committed opponents, the better your chance of negotiating a settlement.

5. Negotiated Settlement

If you have played your cards right so far, your case is now locally famous. Most people in the district have read about it in the local paper, they've seen your placards and posters and parades and car stickers, they've been handed leaflets while shopping on Saturday morning and been called on to sign the petition. They've even read about you in the national papers. But they are not quite sure who is against you except 'the council' or 'the ministry', since no one has come out unequivocally to say the plan is an excellent one and must go through.

This is the best basis for your second diplomatic offensive. The first requirement is to show that you are going on from strength to strength: you cannot negotiate from a base of exhaustion and desire to call it a day. So your activities must continue on the assumption that the next inevitable stage is the public inquiry.

In fact, you do not want a public inquiry if you can possibly win without one. But nor do the enemy: it means enormous work, the preparation of endless documents, fierce scrutiny of all their previous work by men whose judgments may determine their future careers. If they suspect that you cannot afford one, or that your movement has run out of steam, they will be encouraged to go on, so do not give them grounds for any such suspicion.

You can now start more direct political action. If the question, 'Would you vote for a candidate who opposed the plan?' receives encouraging answers, now is the time to make the results known, either publicly at the press conference or by private circulation. You can start organizing your own candidates for the next local election, or adopting any who come out on your side. But your chief activity is diplomatic and behind the scenes.

As before, give all uncommitted people a chance of glory. Never say to the press, '. . . we've shown them they can't get away with it . . . frightened of our support . . . taught them a lesson . . .' Let them have every bit of credit they deserve. '. . . most statesmanlike speech . . . one of the few councils who really try to find out the wishes of the people they represent . . . the plan was a valuable exercise . . . the department has behaved most correctly so far . . .'

But people still need a way out, and you must give it to them – publicly, because the face they have to save is their public face. The most common savers are:

- Time. Information, projections, plans, figures, etc. which could not have been known at the time the plan was published. '. . . new ministry standards radically change the cost forecast . . .'; '. . . technical engineering breakthrough just announced which puts alternative projects in a very different light . . .'; '. . . latest figures suggest the curve may be flattening out . . .'
- Personal. If important figures behind the plan have left or been moved, it can be understood that without them the plan will be very difficult to execute, and privately acknowledged (if it is true) that they were the only ones who were really keen on it anyway, and were responsible for all the flaws that are now coming to light.
- Administrative. A reorganization of departments may give an excuse for looking at the plan again and finding things that the old system of organization missed. Defeating the plan then becomes a proof of how much better the new system is.
- Legal. Best of all, investigations may bring to light a rare technicality which suggests that perhaps the authorities would run into trouble in the courts if they pursue the plan: '. . . very unusual combination of facts, no reason why anyone should have thought of it, no one's to blame, lucky we found out in time . . .'

★

However, if the diplomatic moves fail and resolution hardens, you may have to face up to a public inquiry, after all.

PART FIVE

The Decision

I. The Public Inquiry

Hard though you have tried to avoid this, it has been in your mind all along. The legal requirements for a public inquiry are not simple to summarize, but your Legal Cell will have briefed you on them and you should already have organized the necessary support and know the procedure, relevant dates and correct form for registering objections. If you cannot negotiate a face-saving settlement after your counter-attack, the public inquiry is the next stage.

So far you have been conducting a campaign: **from now on you are engaged in a war**. Both sides now start to dig in, to support their positions, and to go over to a war economy. **The war will end with the pitched battle of the inquiry**: it is virtually an action in civil law, except that if it is Sir Humphrey you are fighting – the judge who is hearing the case is in the pay of the other side: you are taking on the civil service, and he is a civil servant. Fortunately, however, Britain has a civil service which is so large and so full of internal rivalries that he may be more kindly disposed than you would guess.

Nevertheless you have a big job on your hands, and it falls mainly on two cells. First the experts: the inquiry is fought according to the rules, not by publicity or negotiation or political pressure, and the experts' labours over the past month are the foundation of your war effort. They will have to prove that the plan you are fighting is faulty and inadequate, and that the alternative is better for everyone: it is the work they have been engaged on since the start. But for the inquiry they will need efforts and expertise beyond their own resources – consulting engineers, forestry experts, environmental consultants, authorities on any number of subjects. You may not need to brief counsel; if you are fighting a superstore, for example, you may get away with an environmental consultant. But if you are opposing an airport or a motorway you will have to retain a barrister if you want to give yourselves a real chance. And for this the fund-raising cell is your only hope.

Up till now you have fuelled your campaign with enthusiasm, dedication, invention, ingenuity, improvisation, and a few hundred pounds collected in small sums. Now you will have to find a five-figure sum, and only your fund-raisers can supply it. This does not mean you do not raise every penny you can from door-to-door collections, bring-and-buy sales, garden fetes, auctions, the Rotary and the WI and the Chamber of Trade: only that you cannot look to them for more than 20 or 30 per cent of the total.

The irony is that if you put in enough time, and effort, skill and money, you have a very good chance of finding an alternative site or route which is in fact an improvement on the original plan: a lot of people agree that the final M4 route, after six successful objections, is better than the original. This means that six communities have been forced into enormous sacrifices in order to do properly work which the civil servants (also paid by their money through taxes) had bungled; and yet they can get no redress and recover no costs.

That, however, is the rule, and this part of the game has to be played strictly by the rules. The evidence at the inquiry must be based on planning law, and normally follows four sections:

(a) Development design and proposal.

(b) Traffic implications

(c) Retail or (if not applicable) competition impact

(d) Environmental implications.

Although the proceedings have now entered a formal, official stage, the work of the grass roots is not yet over. **It is getting progressively easier for local people to participate in a public inquiry, and there is some evidence that government inspectors are quite swayed by the evidence of the breadth, depth and strength of public feeling. And the evidence given by local people has often won inquiries**.

But the inquiry will take its course along prescribed lines, and trying to affect the outcome by political pressure or publicity will work against you. It is up to your experts and your lawyers now. You can only watch and pray.

2. The Final Round

You may lose the inquiry: if so, there is little likelihood of a reversal. You may win and get the plan scrapped. Either way the battle is over. But there is a third possibility: **since the result of an inquiry is not binding on a government, a finding in your favour may be reversed**.

If this happens, your only hope is to become a national scandal. The local press, the local demonstration and the local television news magazine are no longer enough: the Publicity Cell must now use all its techniques to break through as a national cause célèbre. You must make your town or borough or valley a national byword for the oppression of the ordinary citizen by tyrannical bureaucracy. Your parades must be as ingenious and eye-catching as ever, but they must take place in Whitehall and Parliament Square. You must try and arrange a Sunday theatre evening in the West End, an anthology of poems, songs and speeches about freedom and oppression, and see if someone like Judi Dench or Harold Pinter or Joanna Lumley will star in it. You must parade with your banners and your symbol (now nationally known) at airports, outside the Guildhall, in Downing Street, at the Cup Final – anywhere you can bank on the Prime Minister being filmed or televised. Go particularly for live television, where you cannot be edited out: the *Radio Times*, *TV Times* and the other listings magazines will guide you, and the cameras may even be glad of an original parade and demonstration while waiting for a plane that's late, or filling in before the start of an event.

Now, for the first time, it becomes possible to personalize. Your verdict cannot have been overruled without the personal consent of a minister, even though he was probably acting on the advice of his officials. Consequently you can make him the focus of your campaign. His cartoon can grace your banners, his effigy can start your bonfire on November 5th. Now more than ever you need wit and ridicule and large numbers of supporters to show it is not a small-group vendetta you are conducting.

You are not trying to get him to climb down: **that is not the way government works**. **A climb-down would be a signal to every discontented group in the country that they will get their own way if they only make a big enough fuss**. **But a reshuffle is another matter**. The average life-in-office of a minister is about a year, and in some ministries it is only a few months. Your man may soon be moved on or up or down or out, for reasons which have nothing whatsoever to do with your case. His successor must take up office realizing that your case is a millstone round his neck, and you must now give him a chance to rid himself of it while saving his ministry's face. As before, new facts or considerations, a new study with wider terms of reference, or any other of the formulae of graceful withdrawal should be made available, and he should be offered the chance of appearing nationally as a decent chap, a real democrat, the people's champion.

And if you fail, you fail. And the final irony is that when the bulldozers move in and your community is destroyed, the campaign itself will have ensured that it has become a far more healthy, warm, living, unified community than it ever was before the plan was published.

USEFUL ADDRESSES

Action with Communities in Rural England
Somerford Court
Somerford Road
Cirencester
Glos. GL7 1TW
Tel 01285 653477

Association of Convenience Stores
Federation House
17 Farnborough Street
Farnborough
Hampshire GU14 8AG
Tel 10252 515001

The Association for the Protection of Rural Scotland
Gladstone's Land (3rd Floor)
483 Lawnmarket
Edinburgh EH1 2NT
Tel 0131 225 7013/3
Fax 0131 225 6592

Association of Town Centre Management
1 Queens Gate
London SW1 9BT
Tel 0171 222 0120
Fax 0171 222 4440

Campaign for the Protection of Rural Wales
Ty Gwyn
31 High Street
Welshpool
Powys SY21 7YD

Council for the Protection of Rural England (CPRE)
Warwick House
25 Buckingham Palace Road
London SW1W 0PP
Tel 0171 976 6433
Fax 0171 976 6373

The organisation produces free guides, including: *Responding to Planning Applications, Campaigners' Guide to Public Enquiries and Planning Appeals.* Also *Index to Planning Policy Guidance*

Tel 01938 552525/556212
Fax 01938 552741

Department of the Environment
Publications Despatch Centre
Blackhorse Road
London SE99 6TT
Tel 0181 691 9191 (leaflets) 0171 2276 0900 (enquiries)
Fax 0181 533 1618

Publish a range of free booklets about planning and environment issues, including *Development Plans – What You Need to Know.*

Friends of the Earth
Underwood Street
London N1 7SQ
Tel 0171 490 1555
Fax 0171 490 0881

National Sensitive Sites Alliance
Royston
Gloucester Road
Alveston
Bristol BS12 2QQ
Tel 01454 281586

Opposition to Destruction of Open Green Spaces
(OTDOGS)
6 Everthorpe Road
London SE15 4DA
Tel/Fax 0181 693 9412

Produces *Save Green Spaces from Destruction by Food Giants: A
Practical Guide to Local Action* (1994)

Planning Aid
c/o The Royal Town Planning Institute
26 Portland Place
London WIN 4BE
Tel 0171 636 9107

The Press Association
292 Vauxhall Bridge
London SW1

Rural Development Commission
Stone Hall
High Street
Wallingford
Oxon OX10 0DB
Tel 014918 32116

For a selection of printers producing competitively priced leaflets and stationary, as well as companies supplying promotional

items custom-printed with logos, including mugs, T-shirts, pens etc. the classified pages of the fortnightly publication *Exchange and Mart* are an excellent starting point.